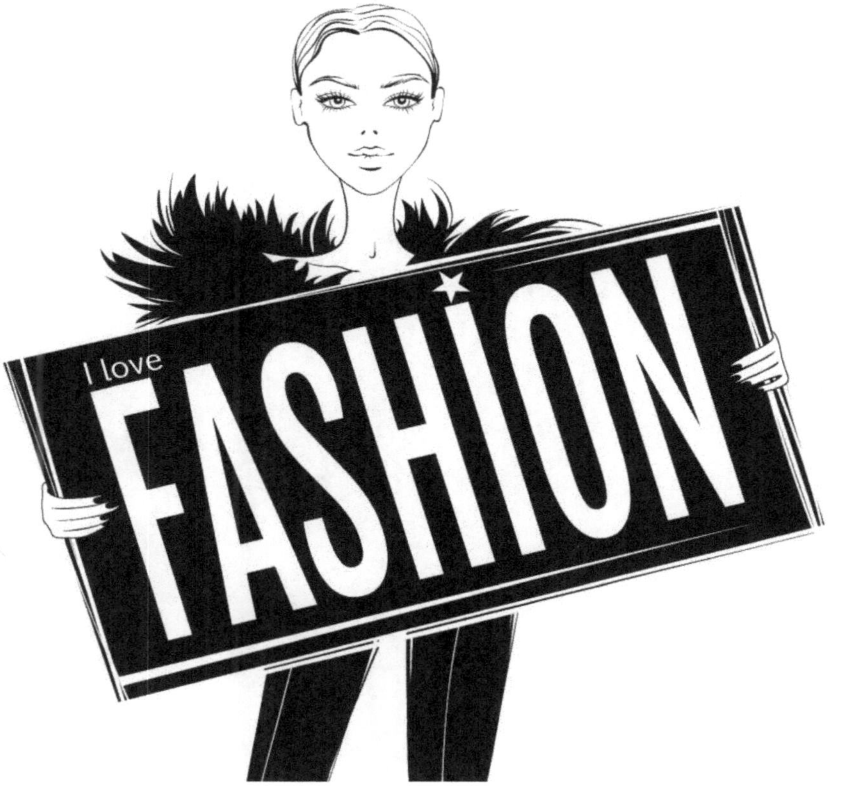

Belongs to:___________________________________

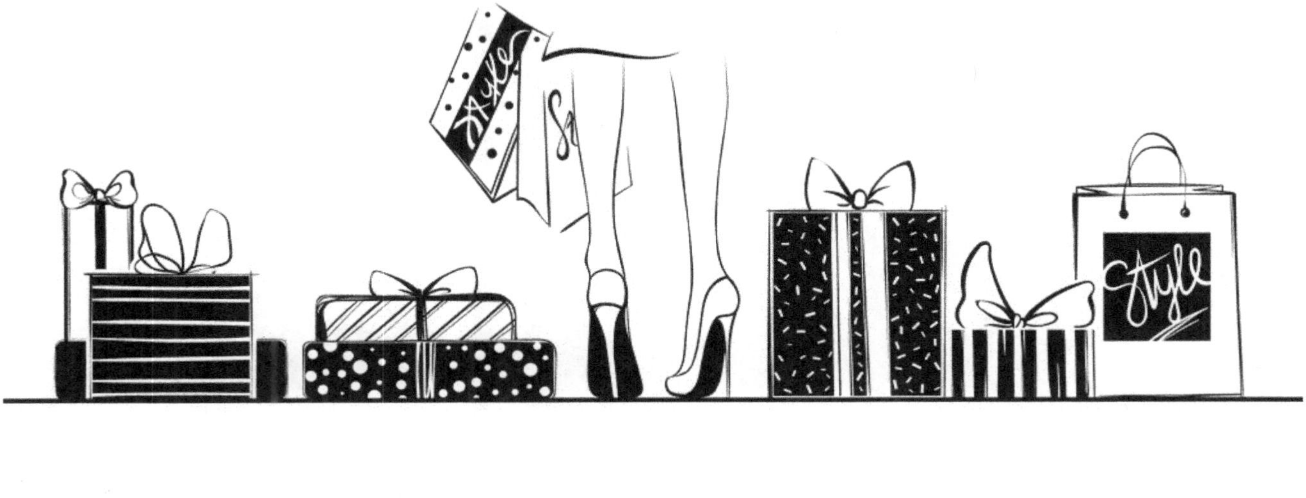

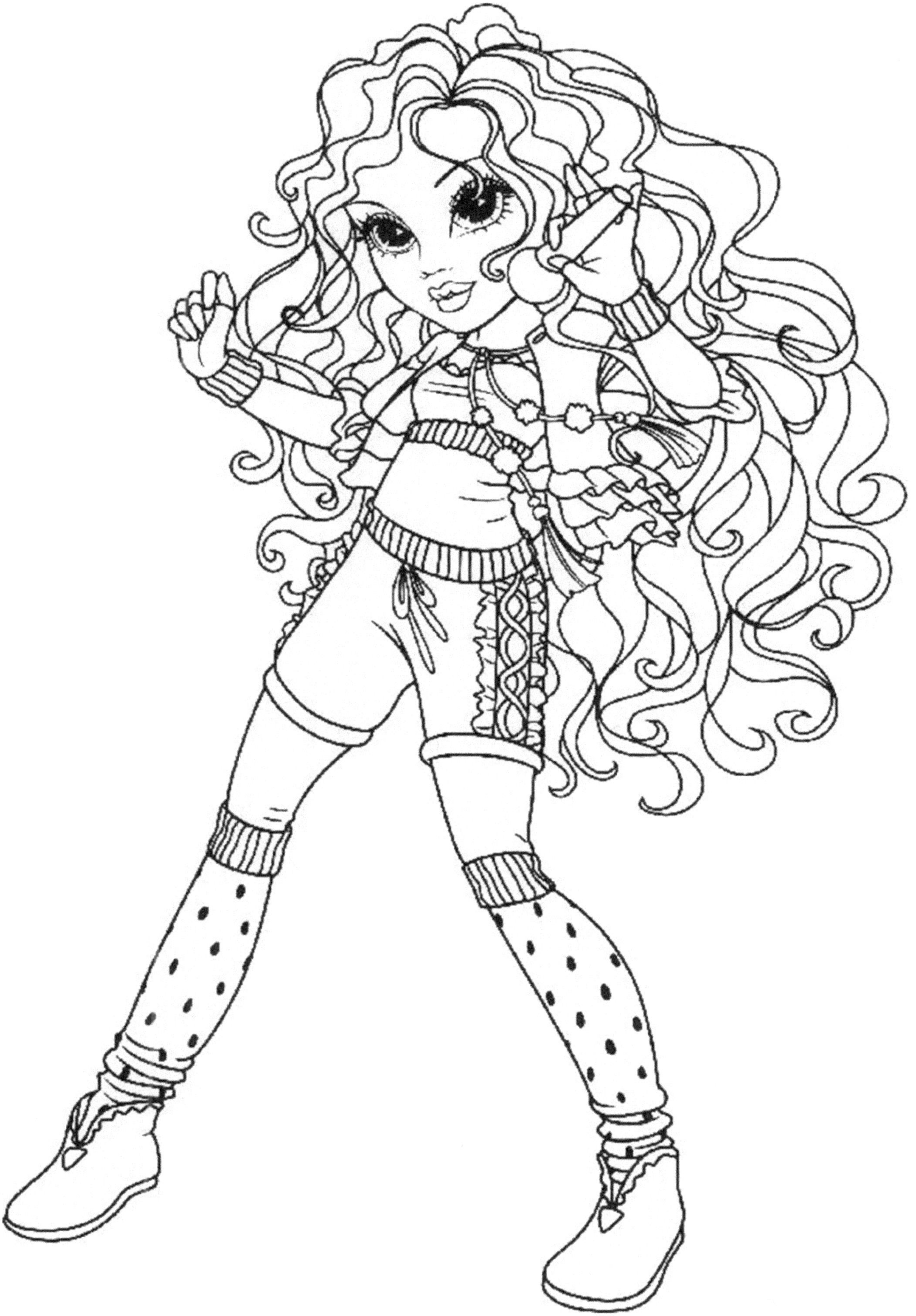

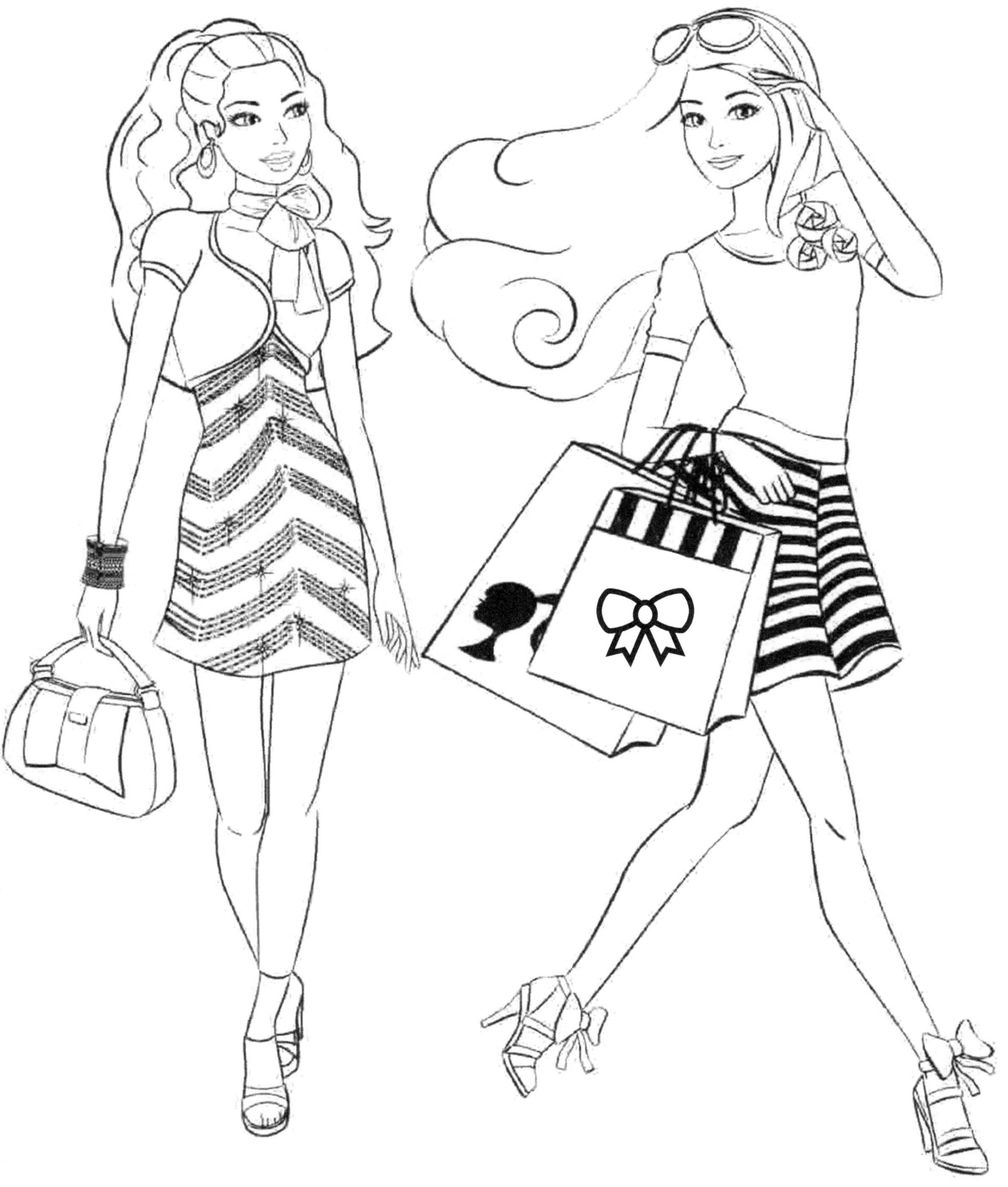

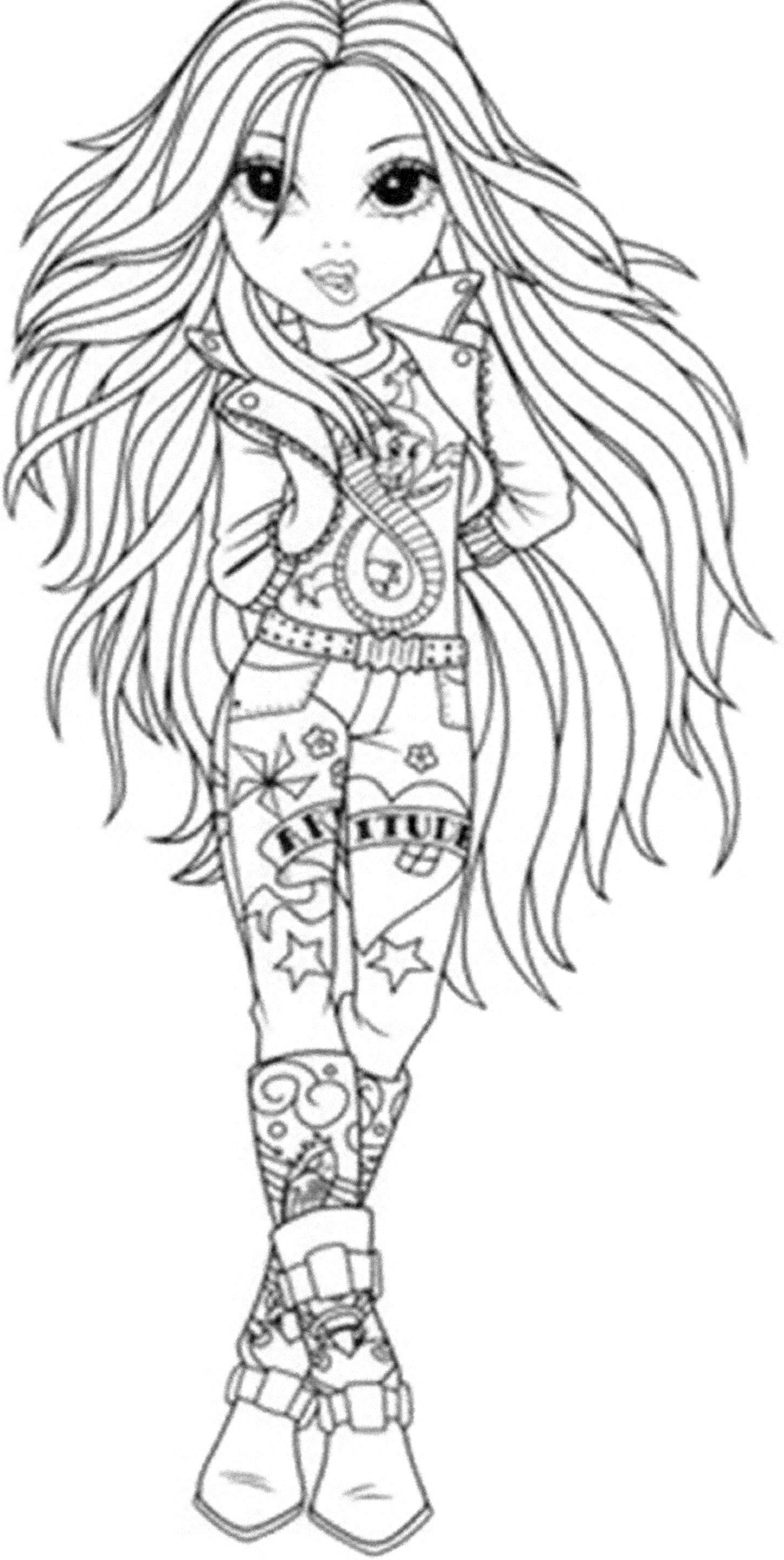

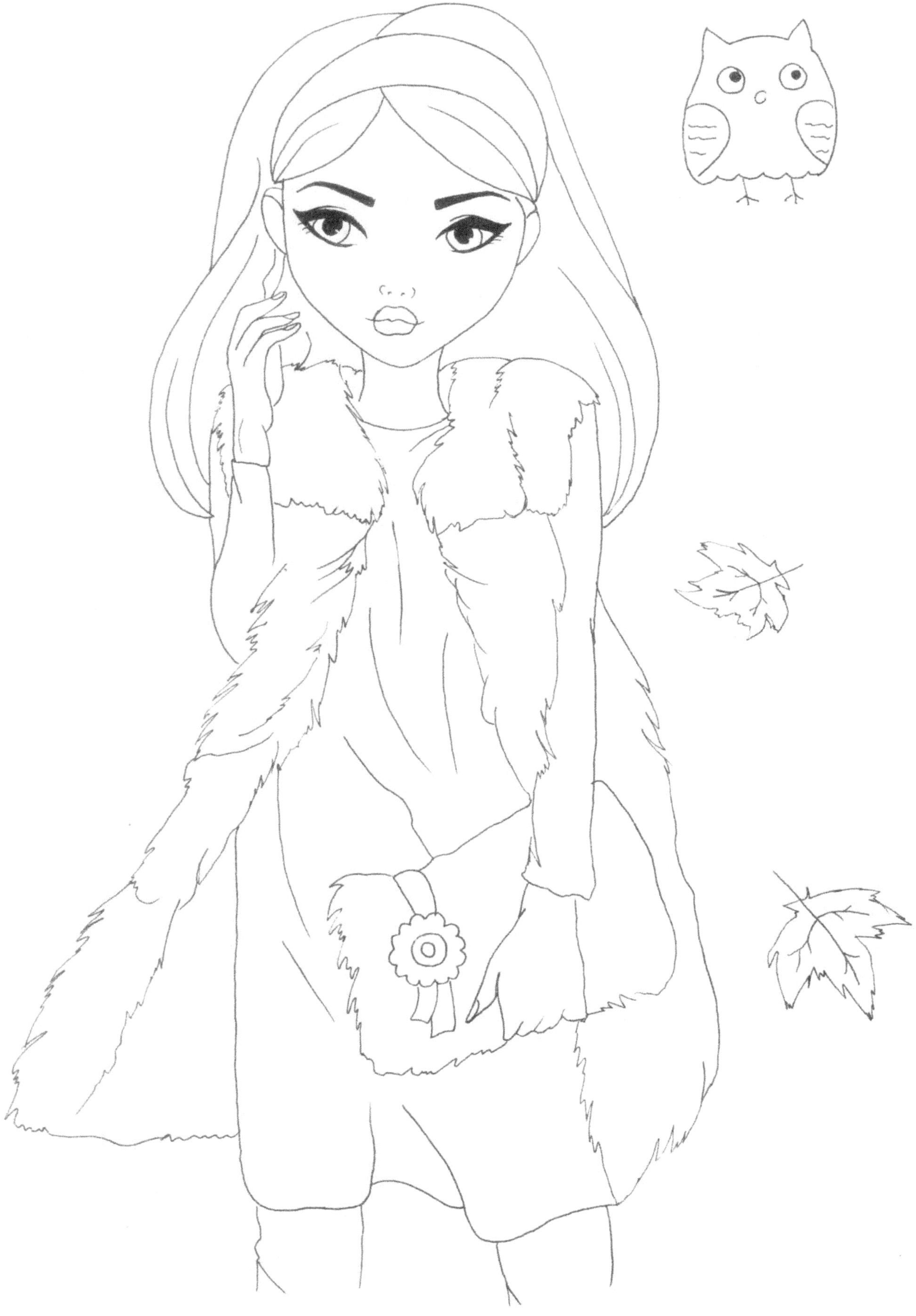

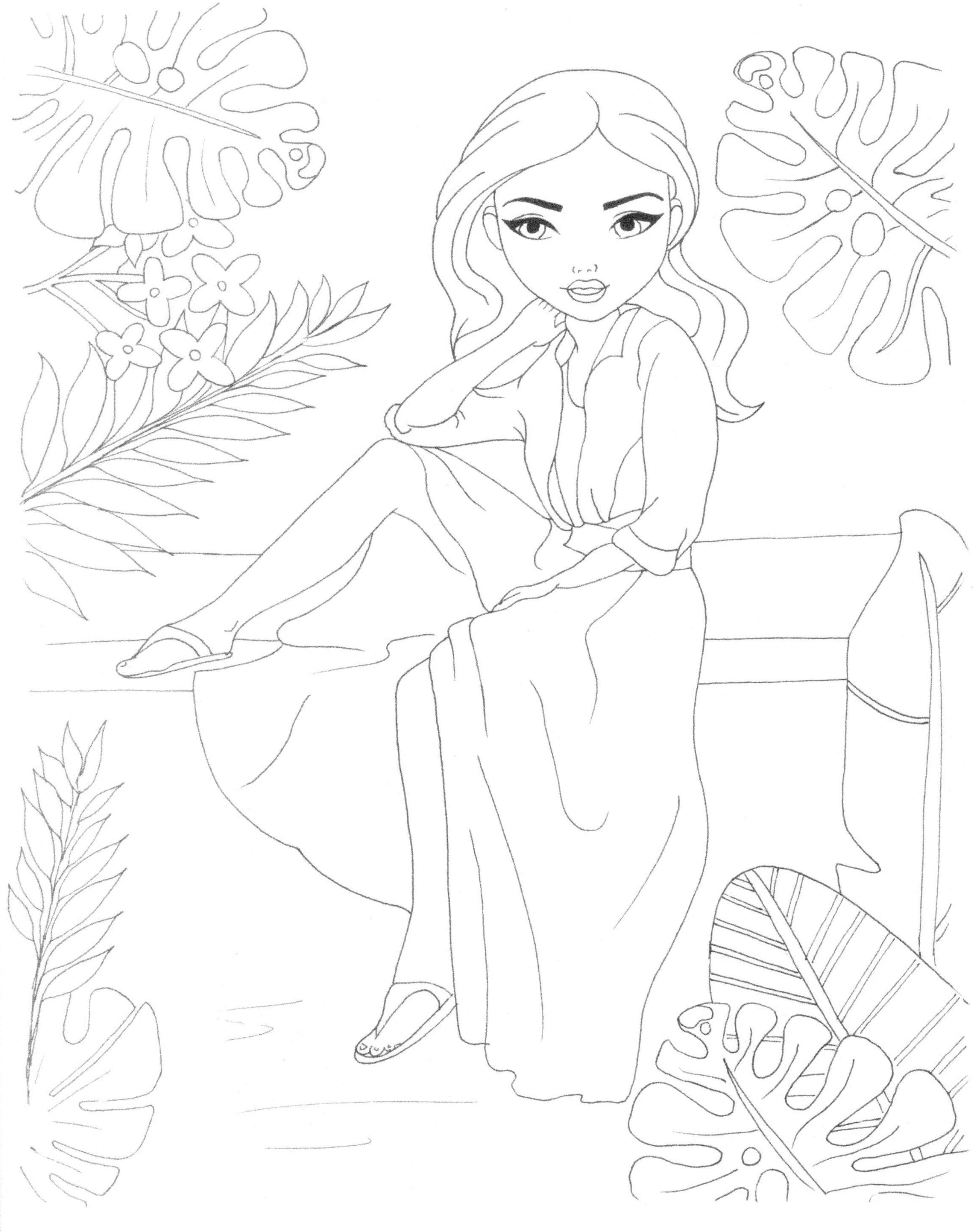

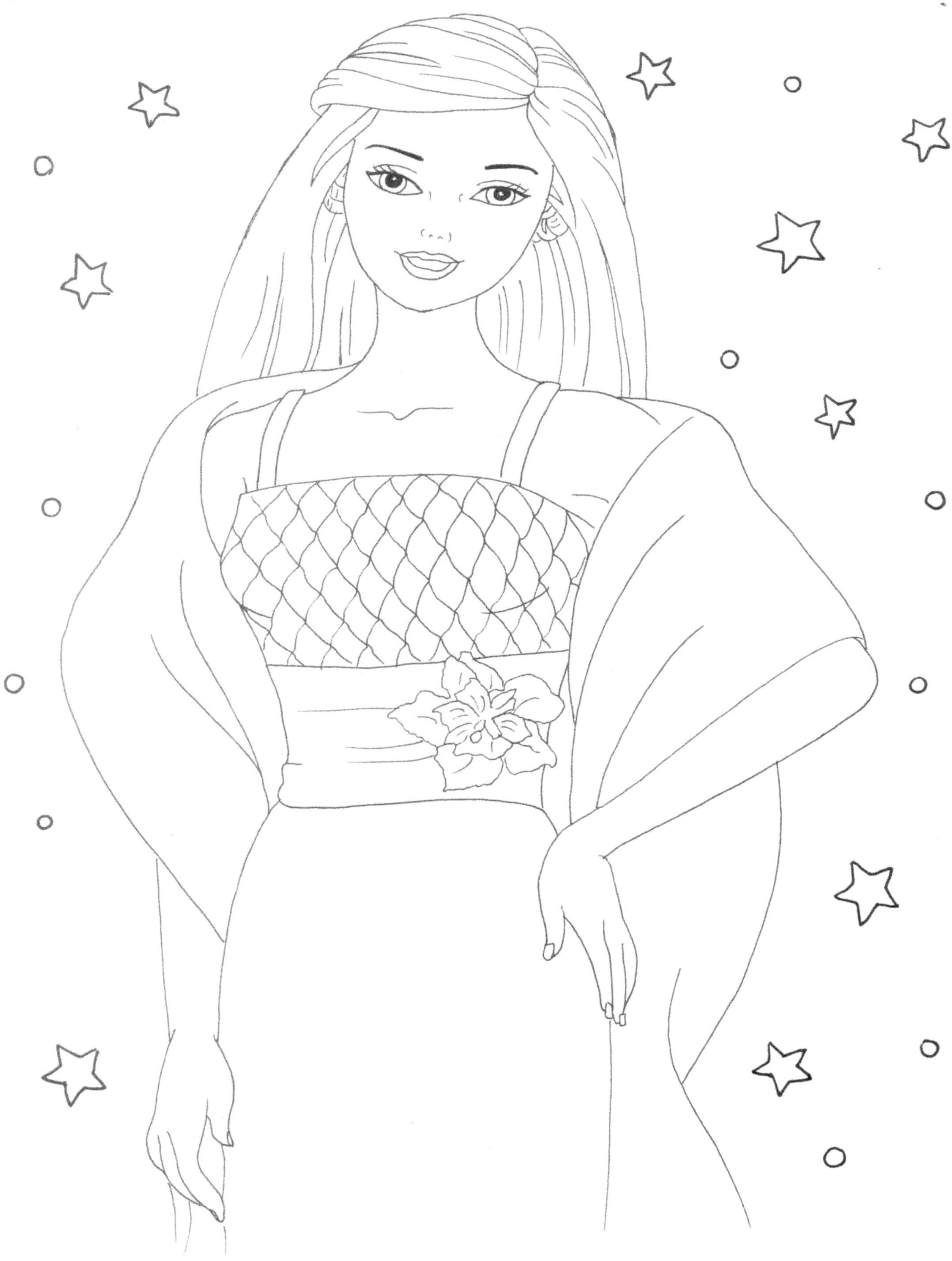

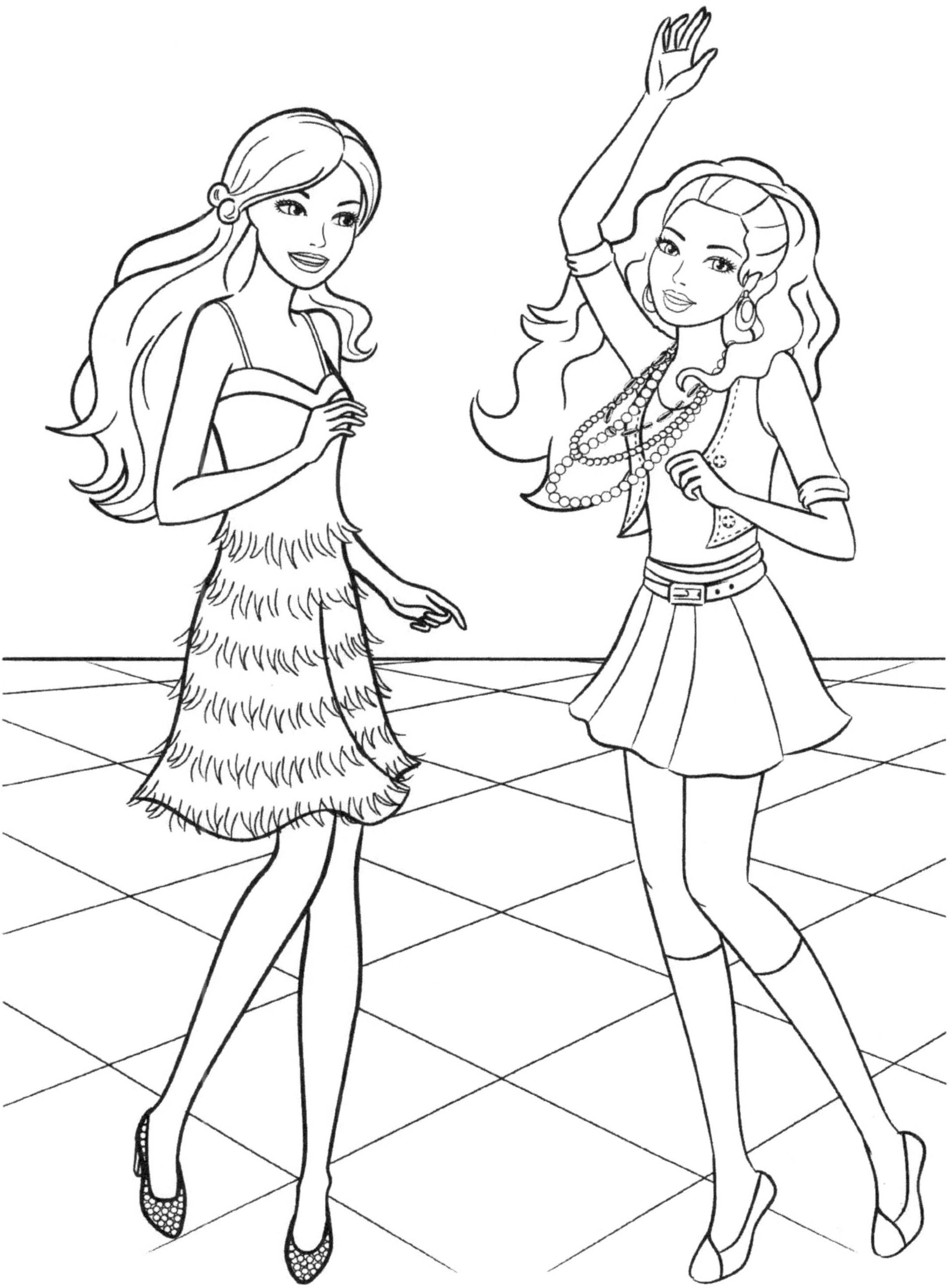

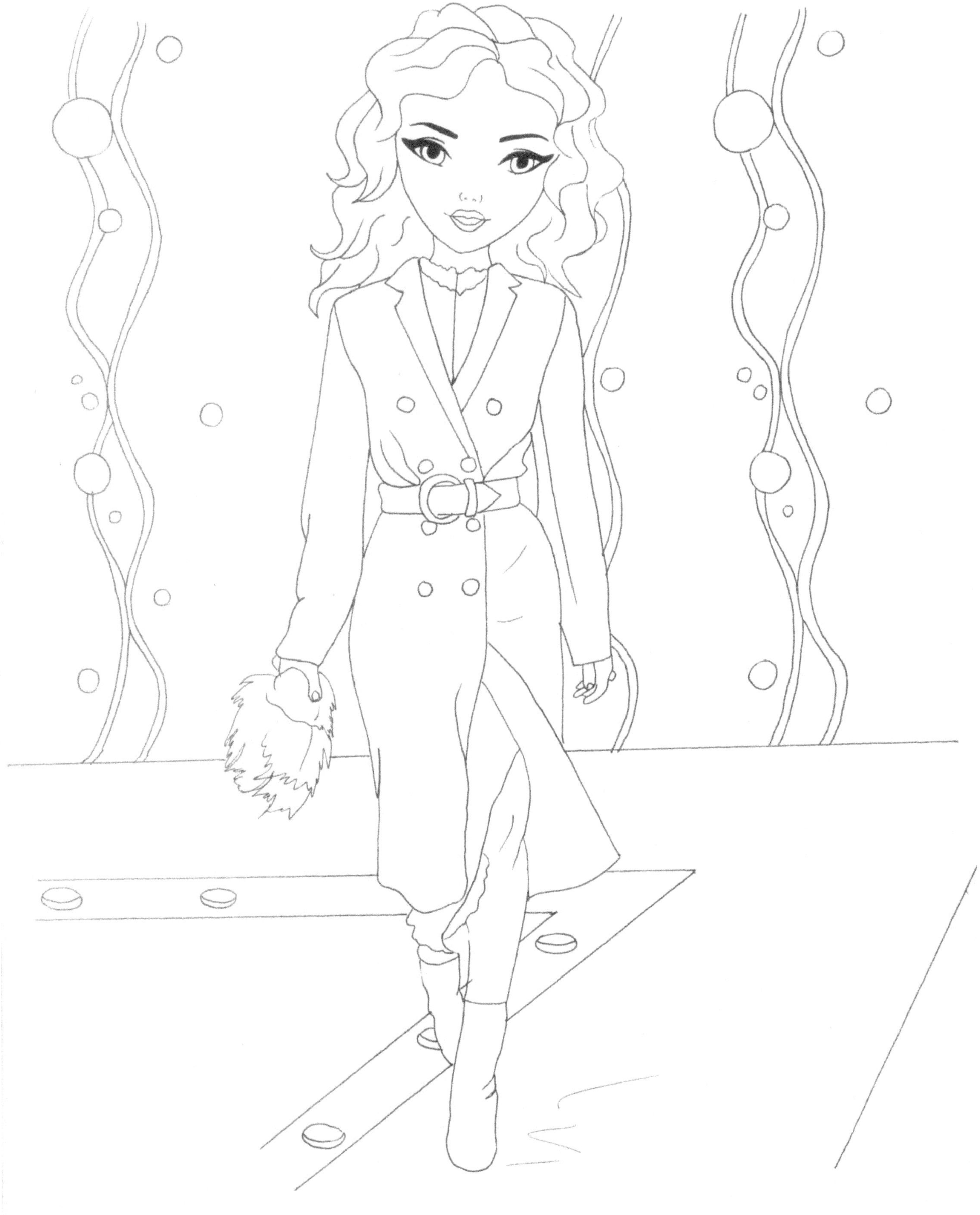

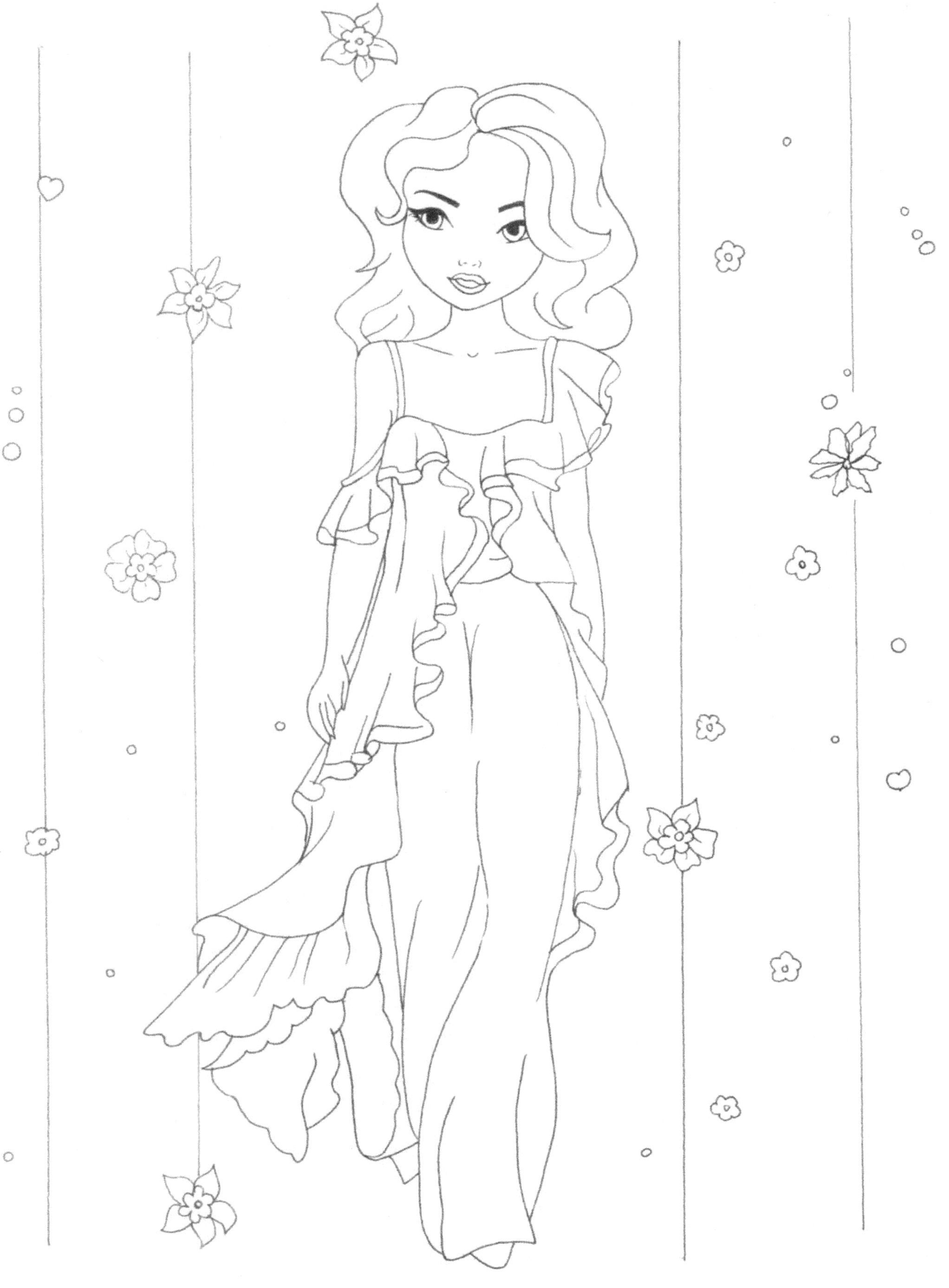

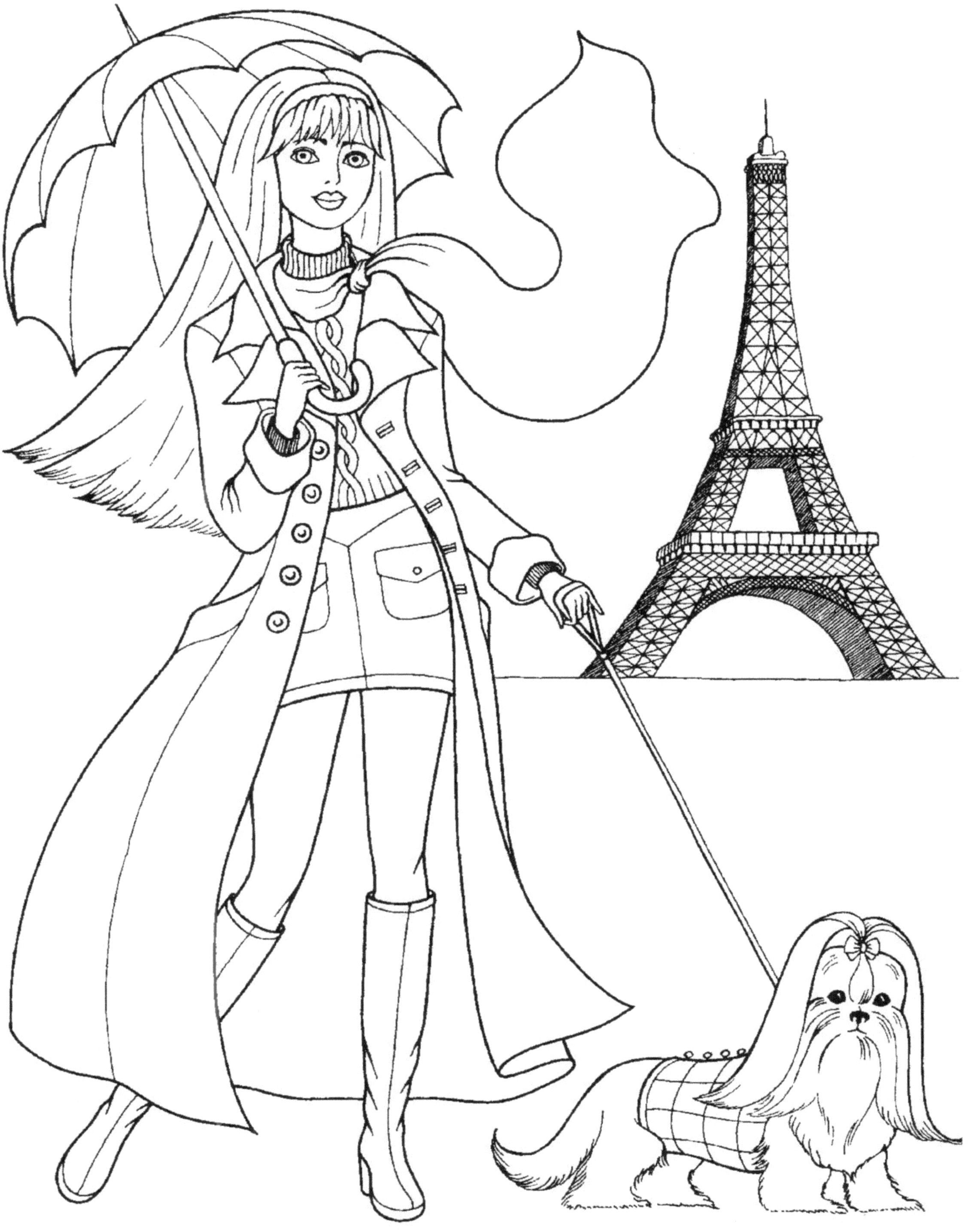

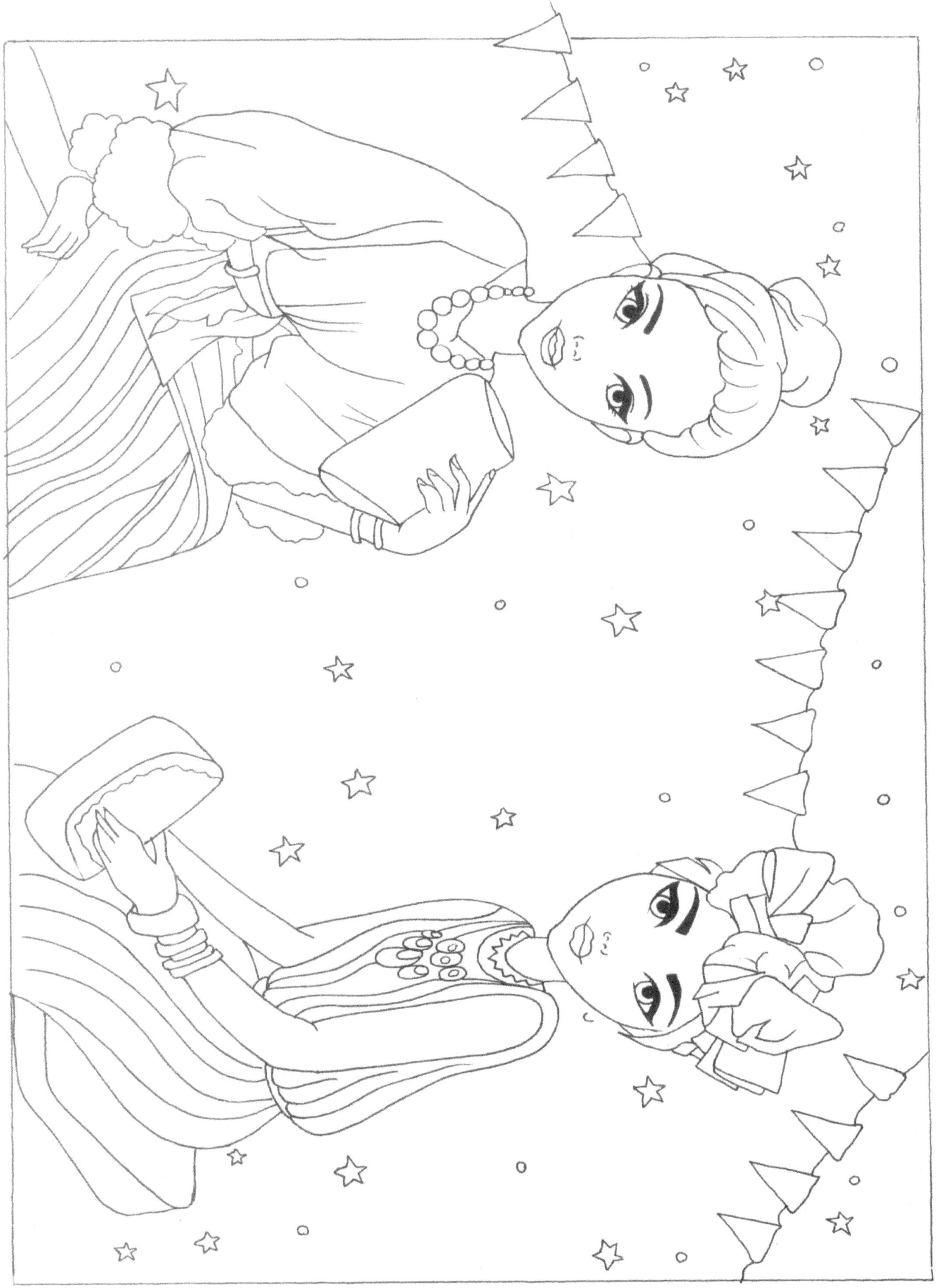

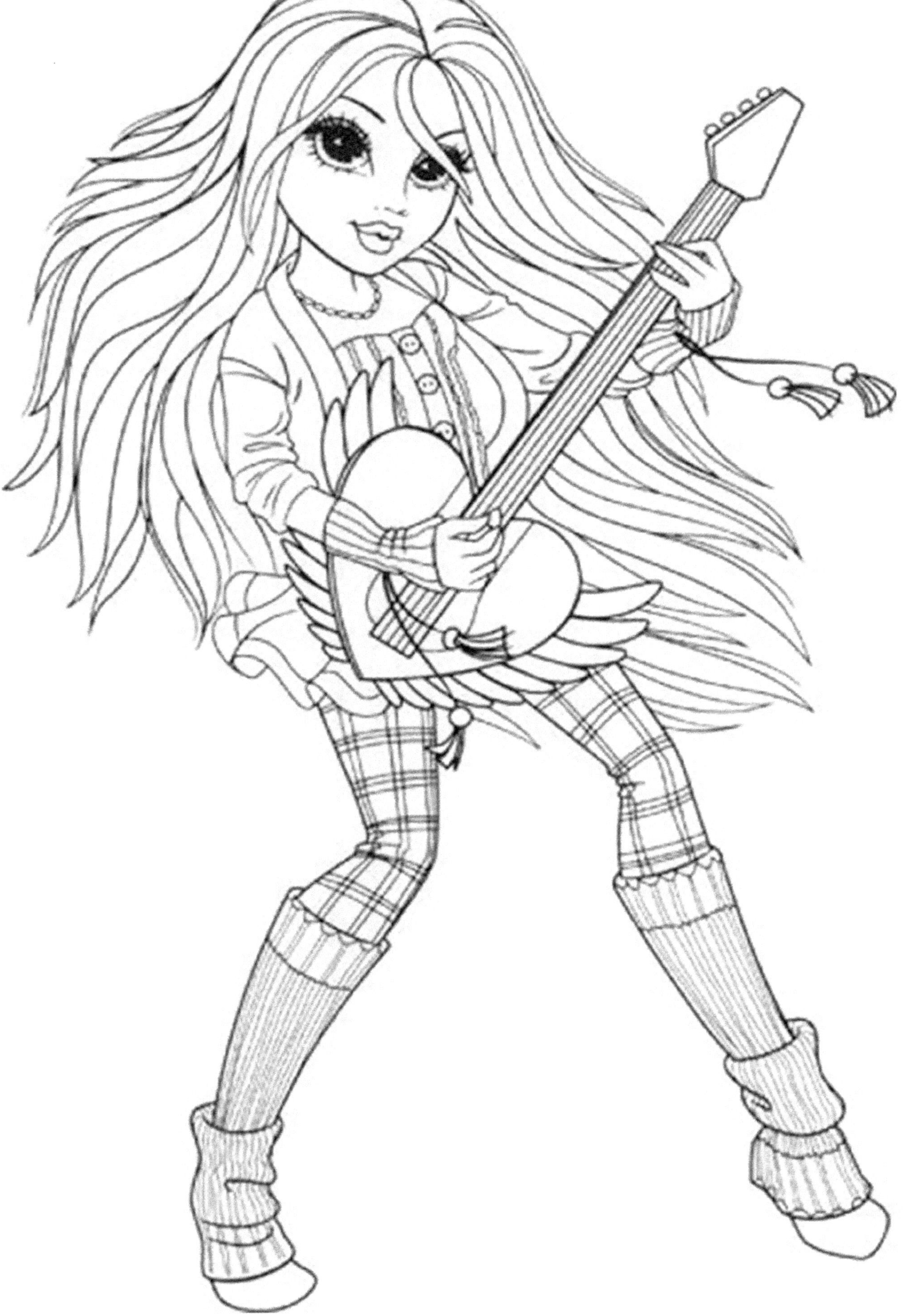

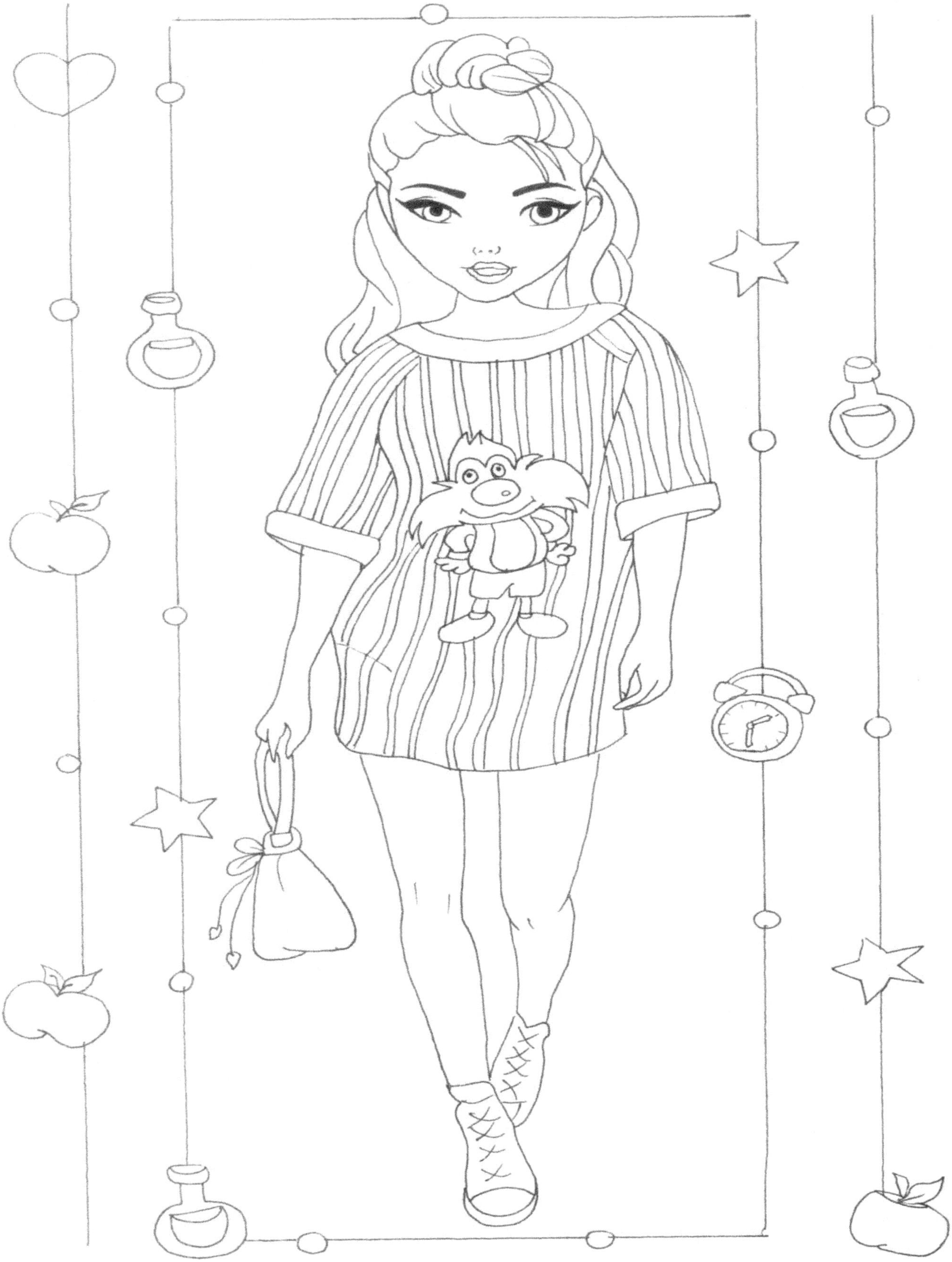

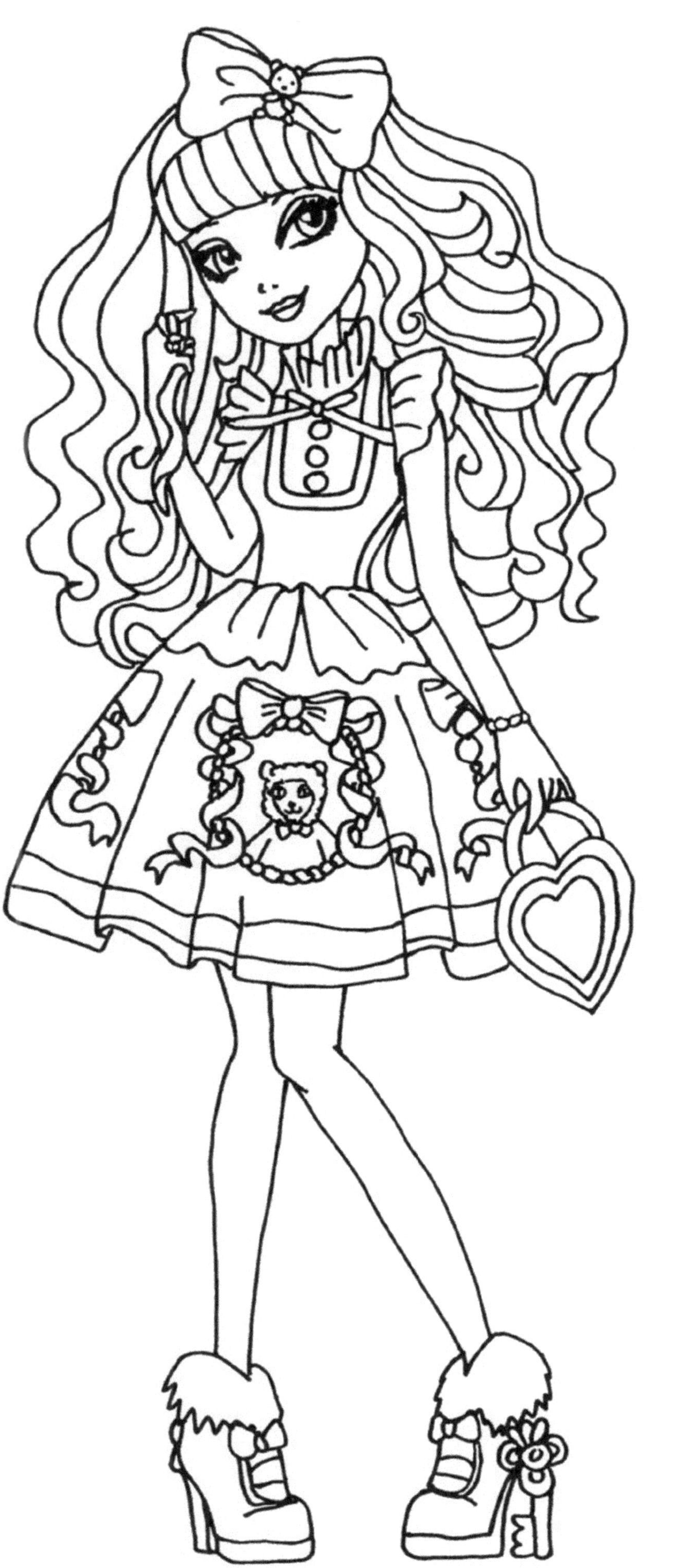

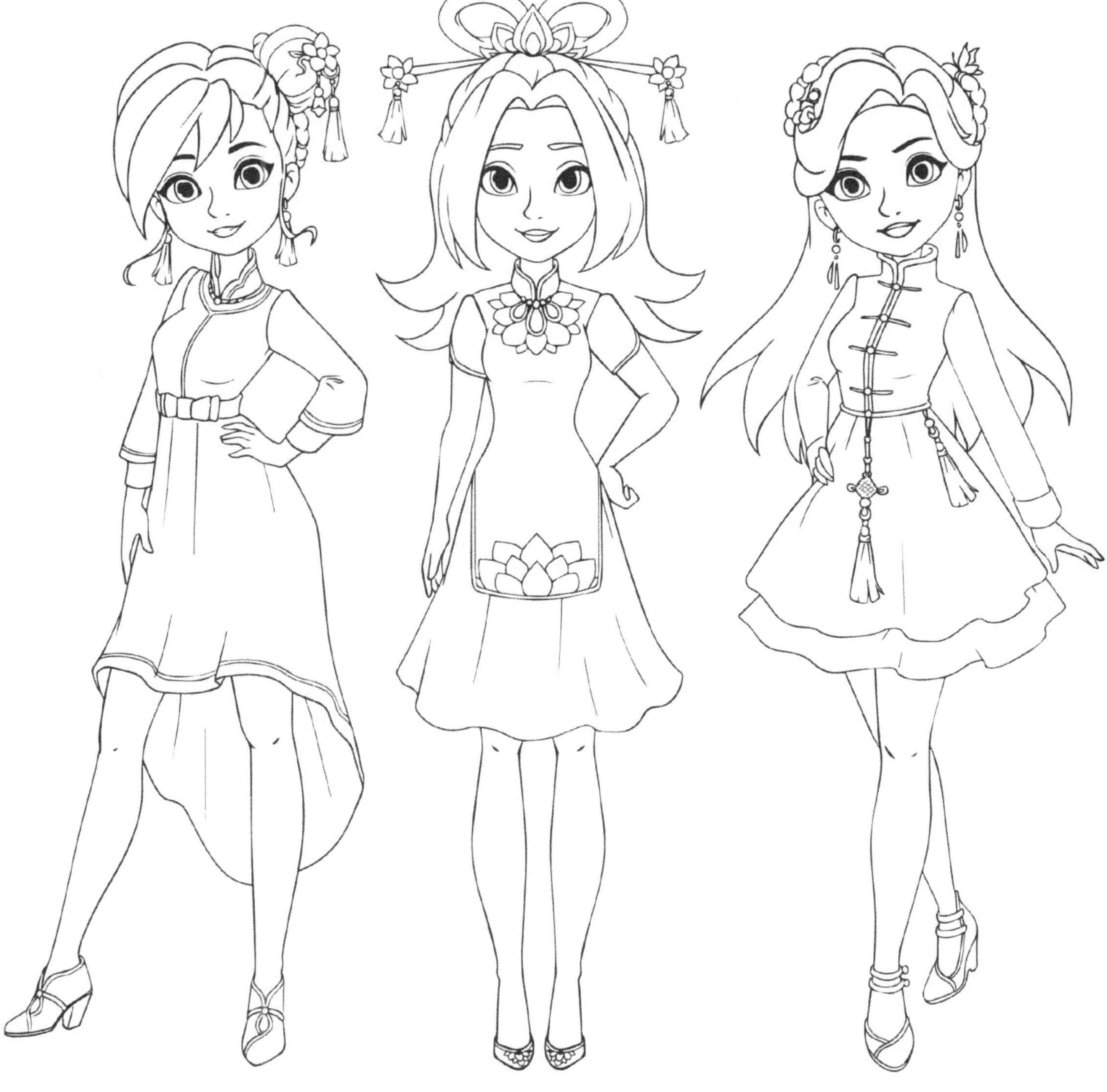

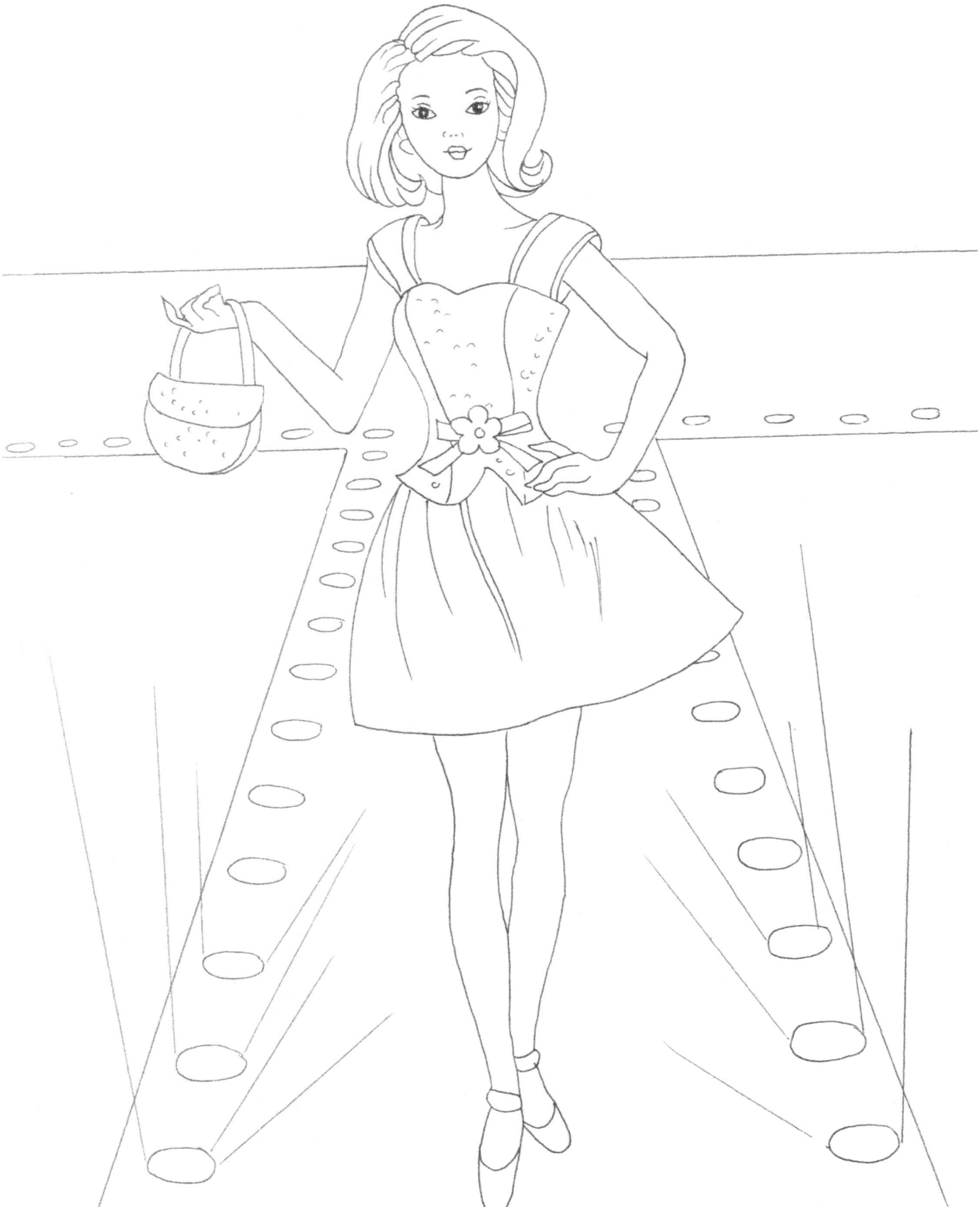

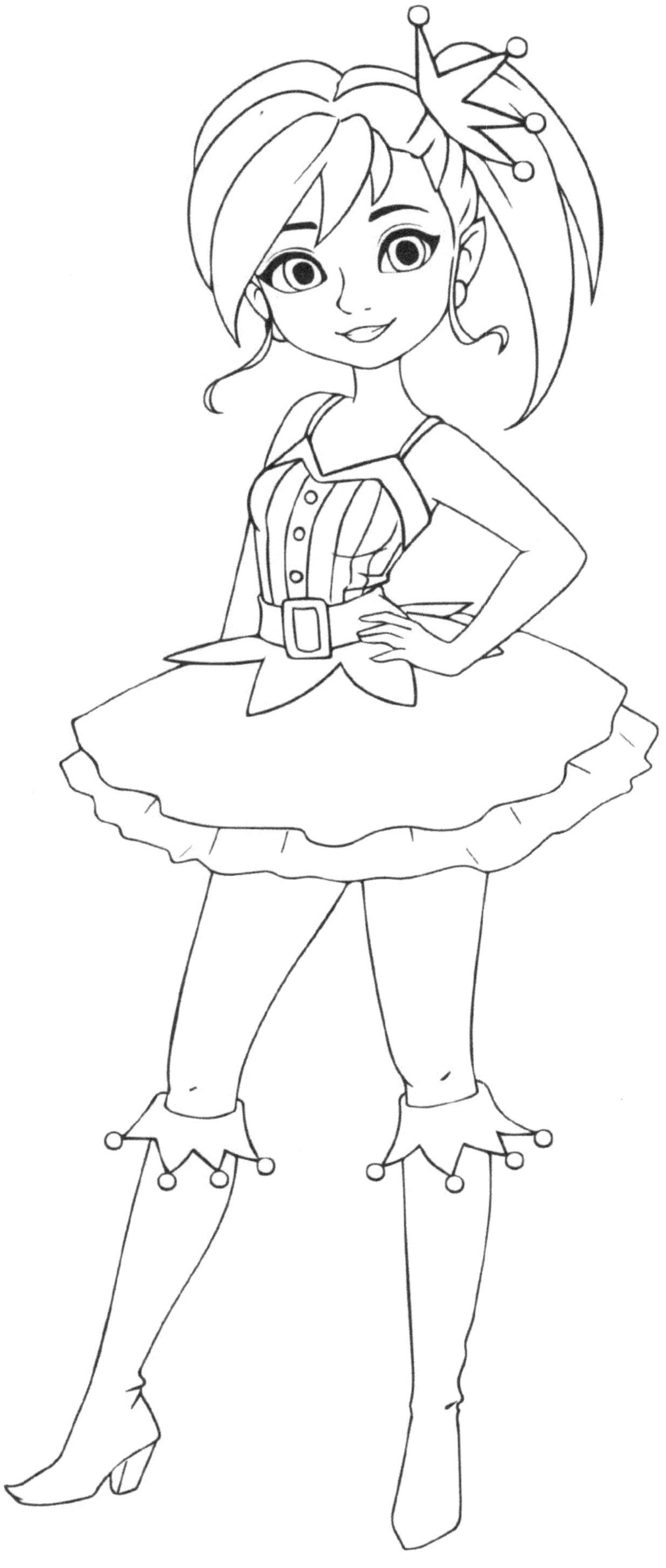

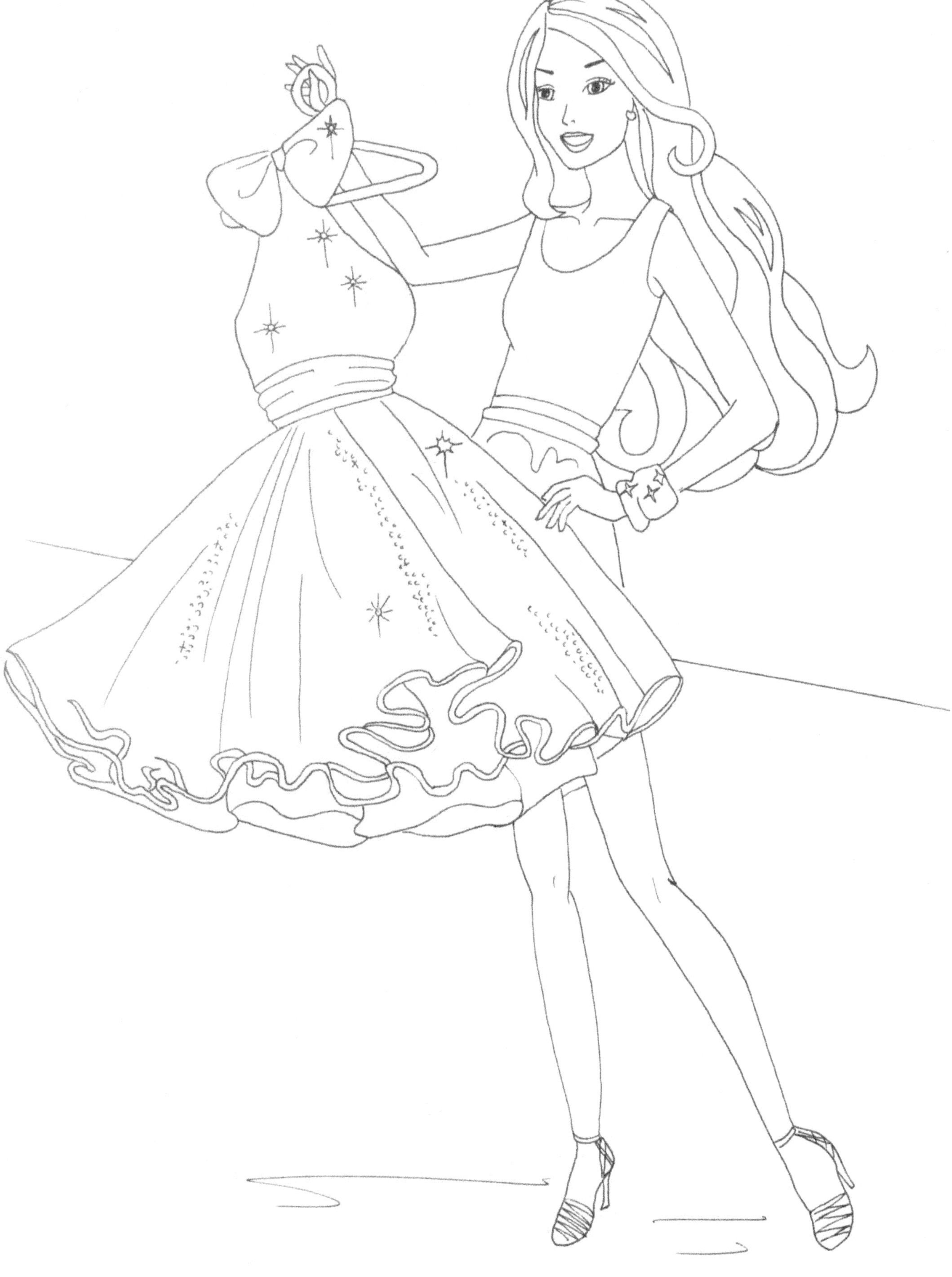

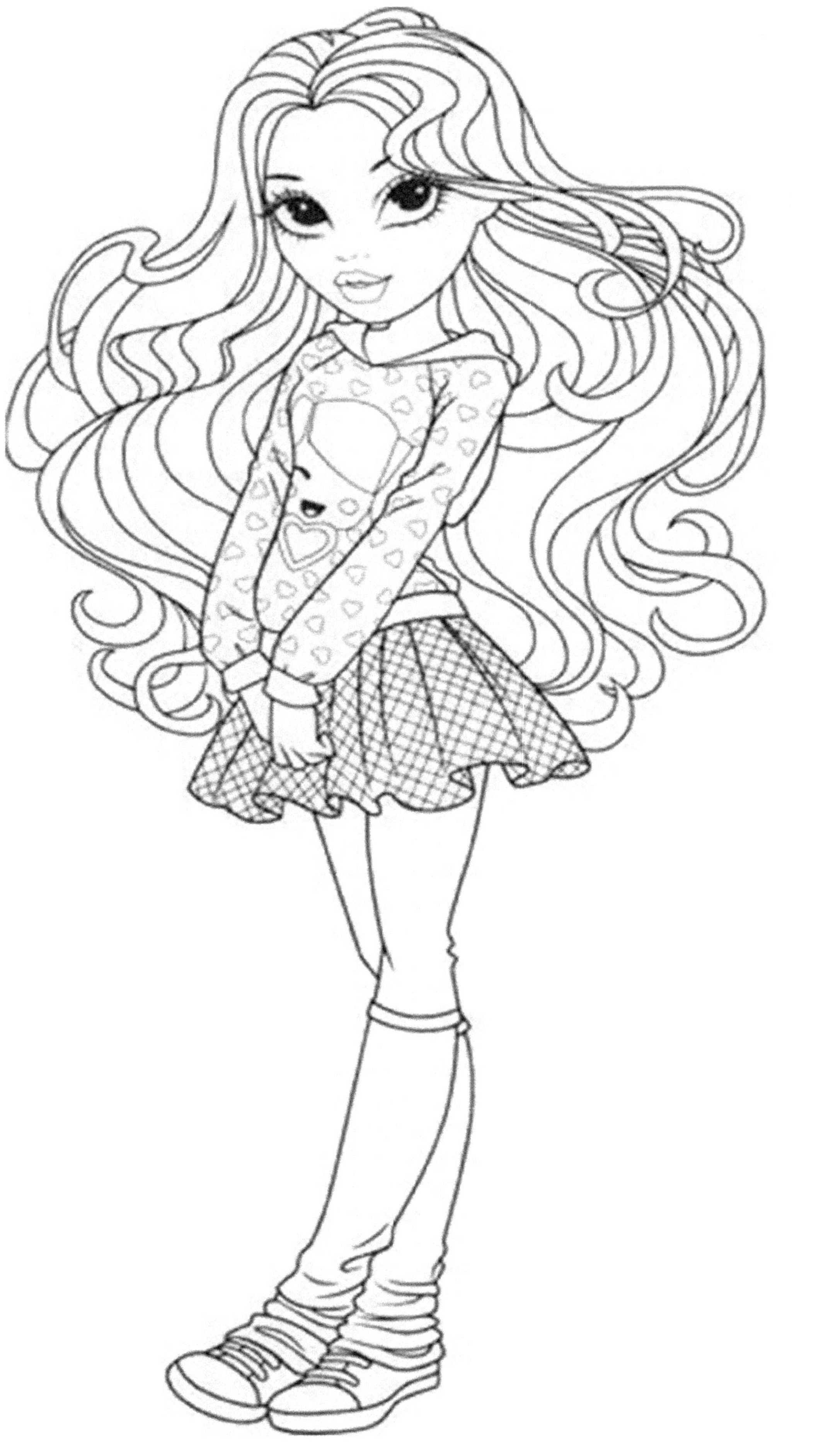

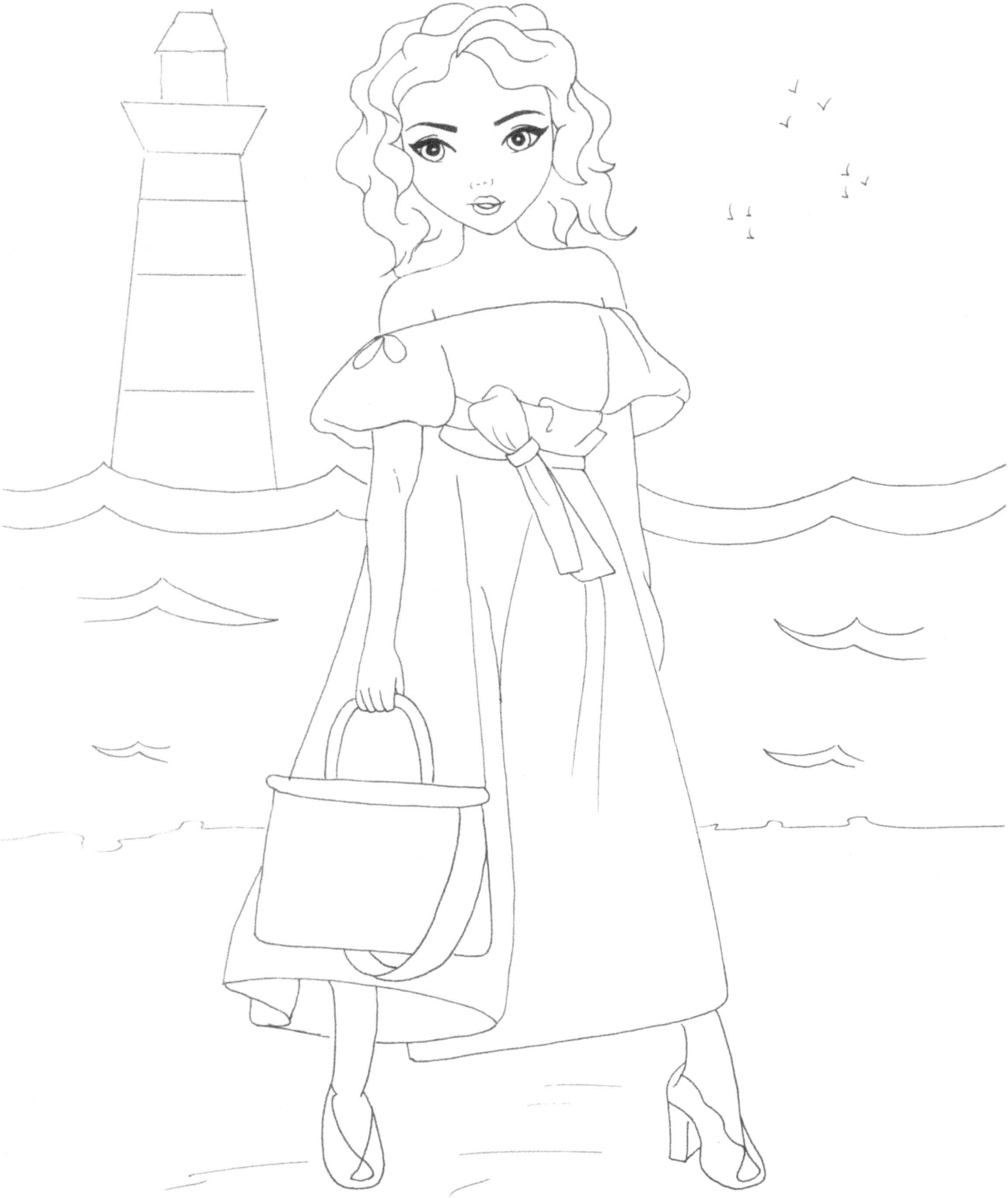

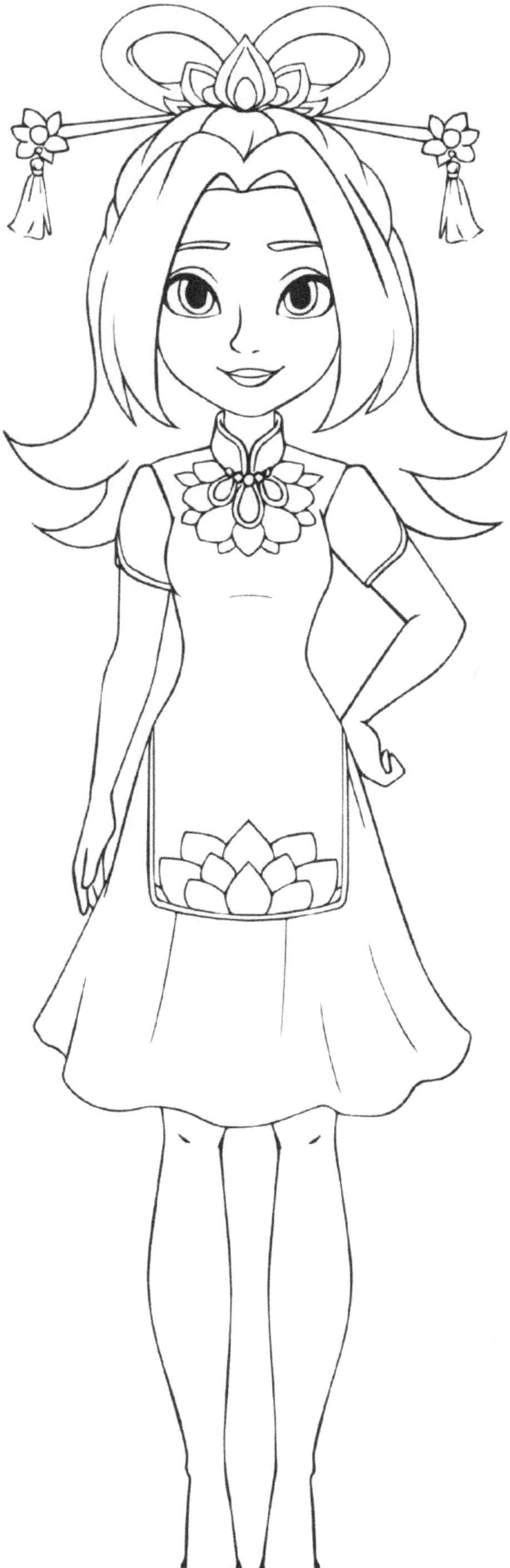

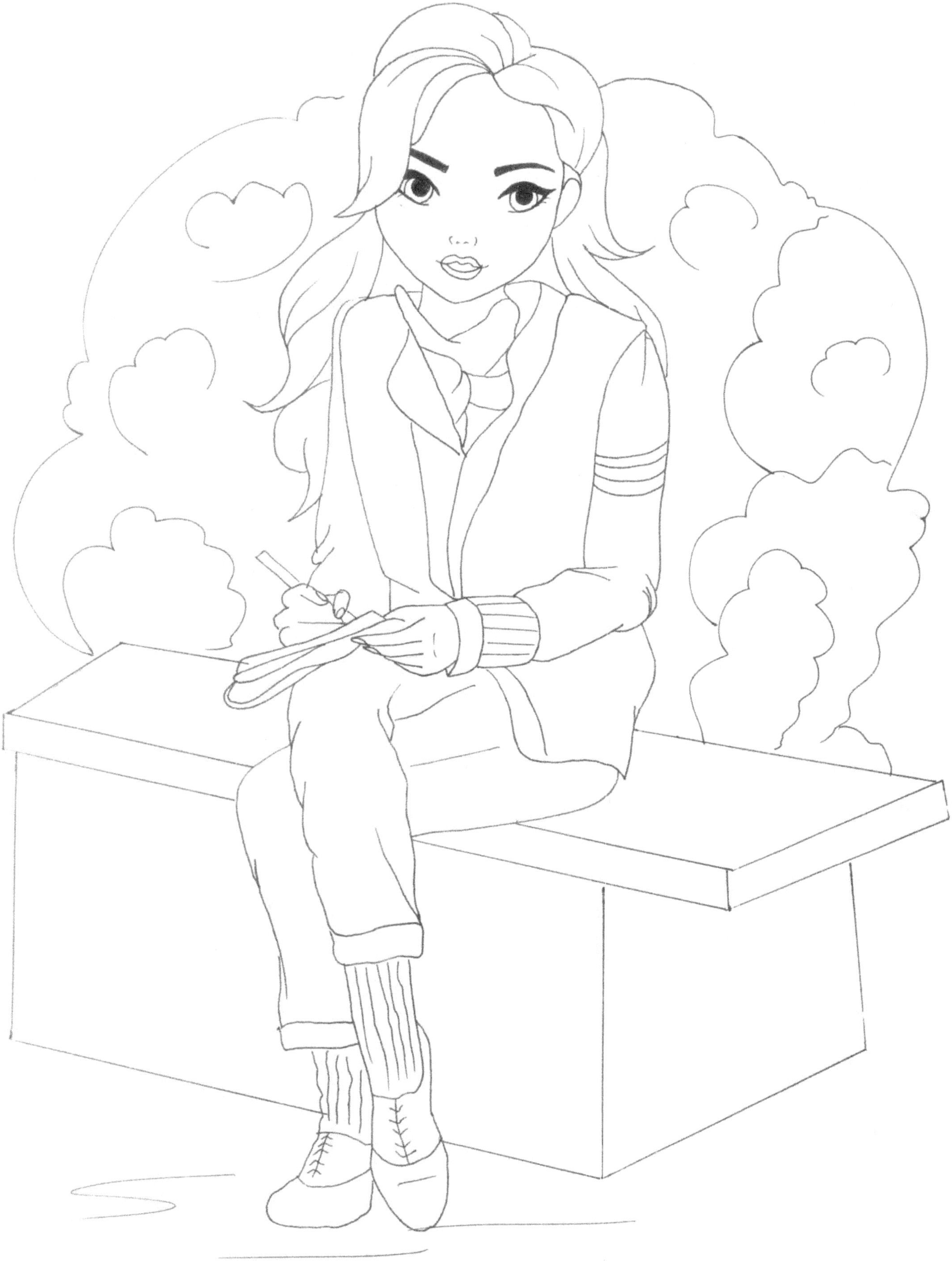

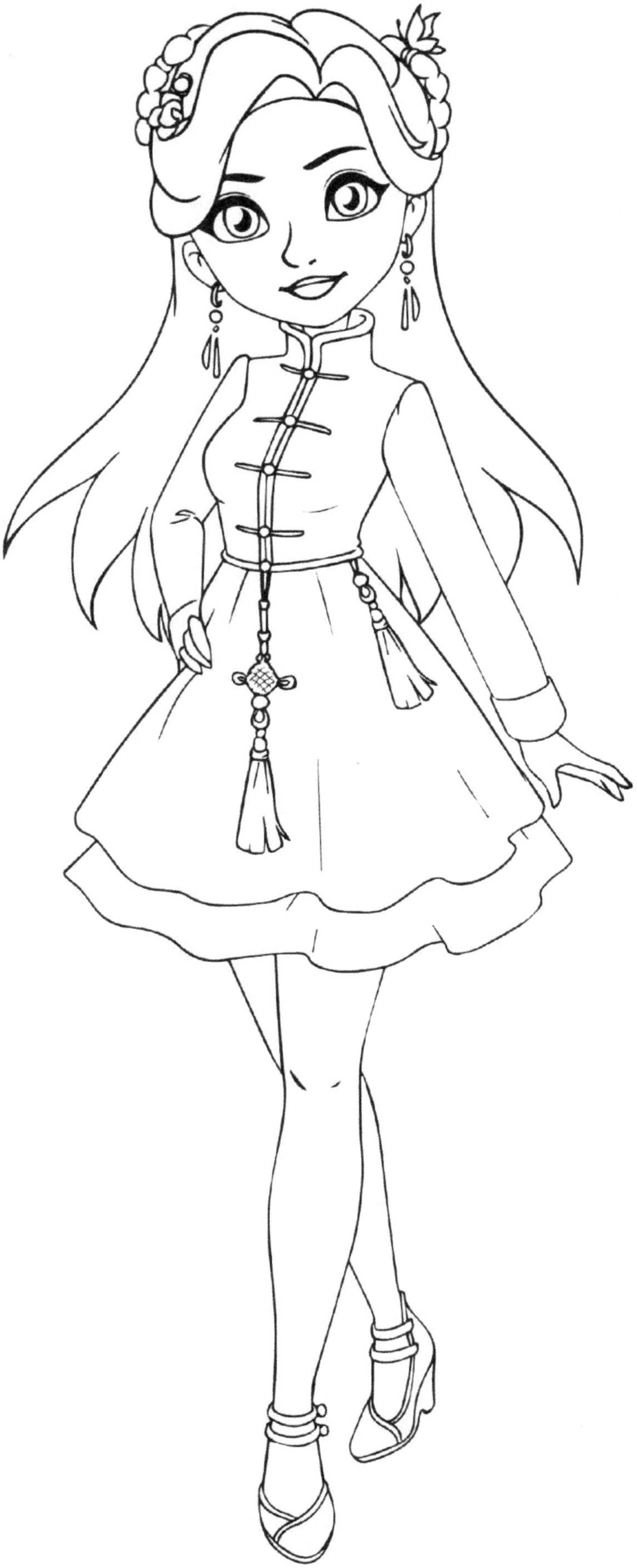

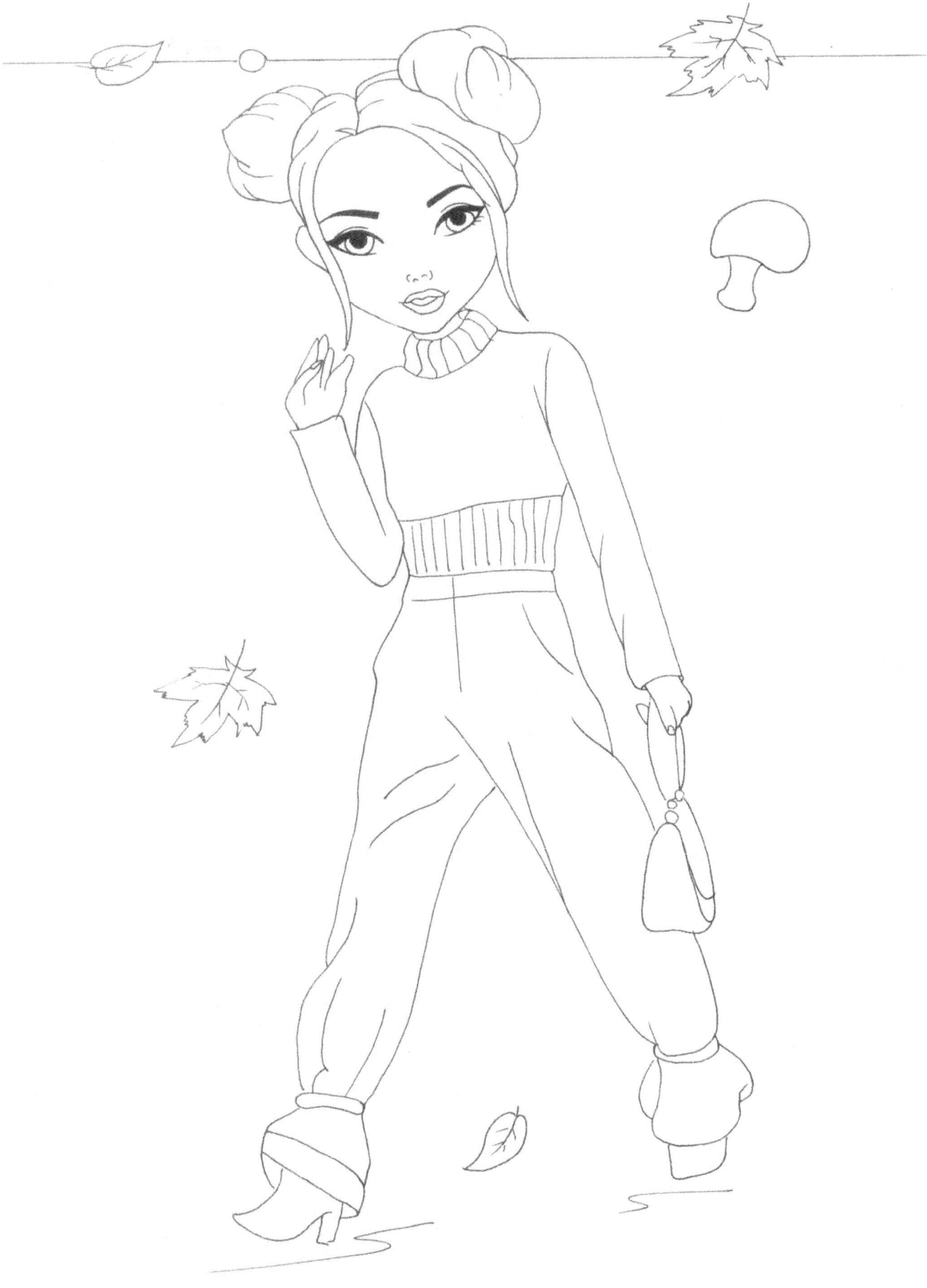

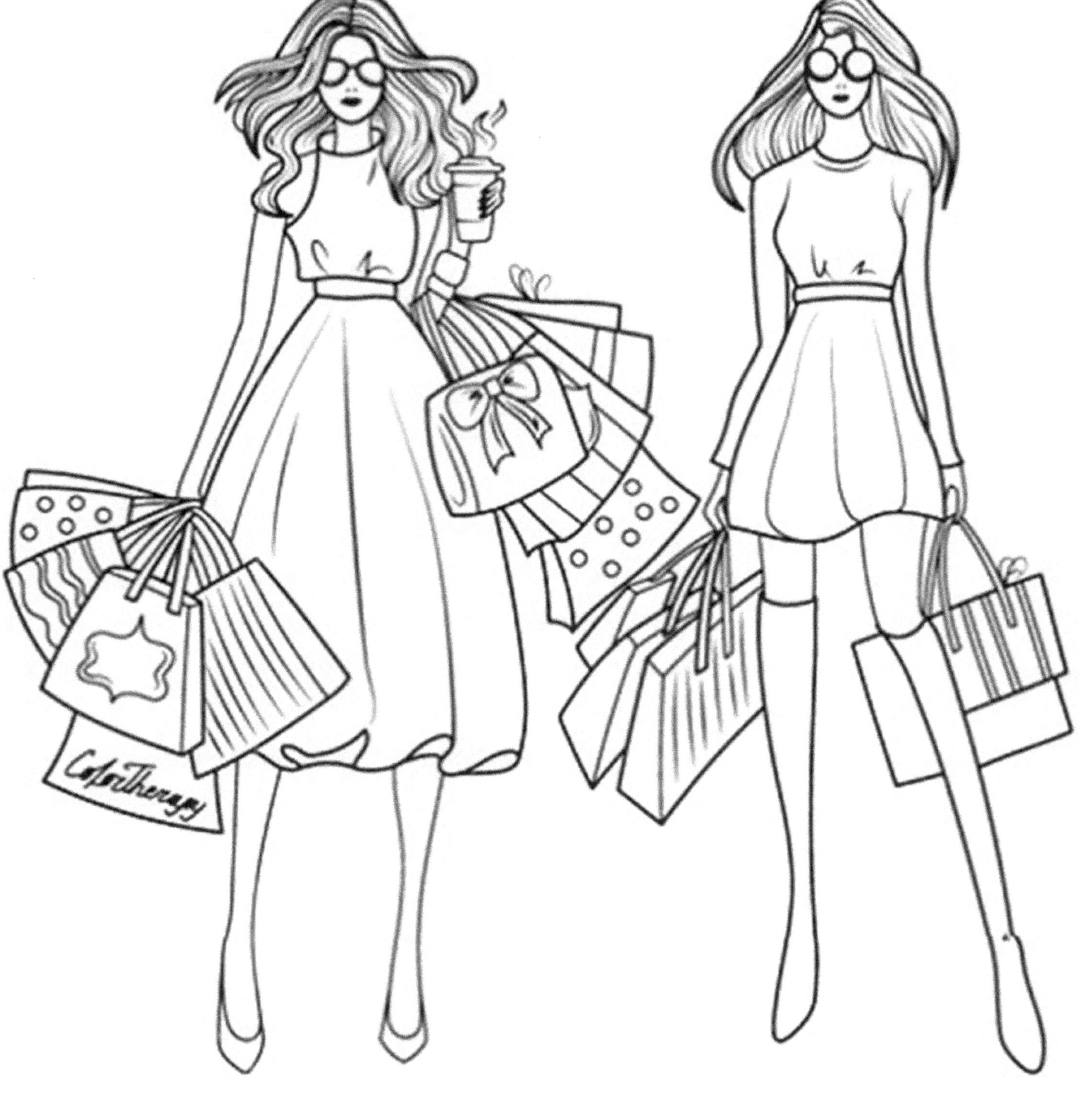
ColorTherapy

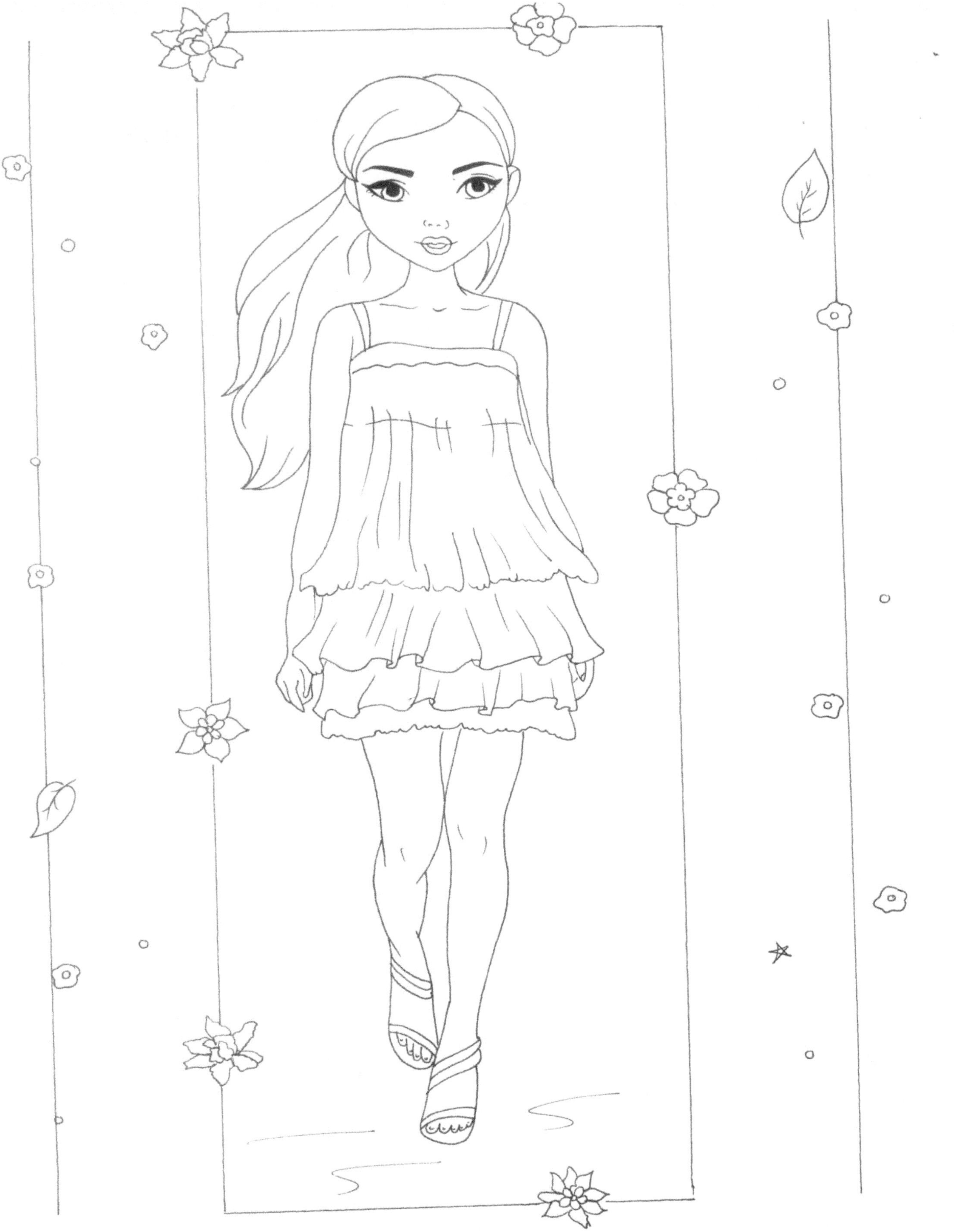

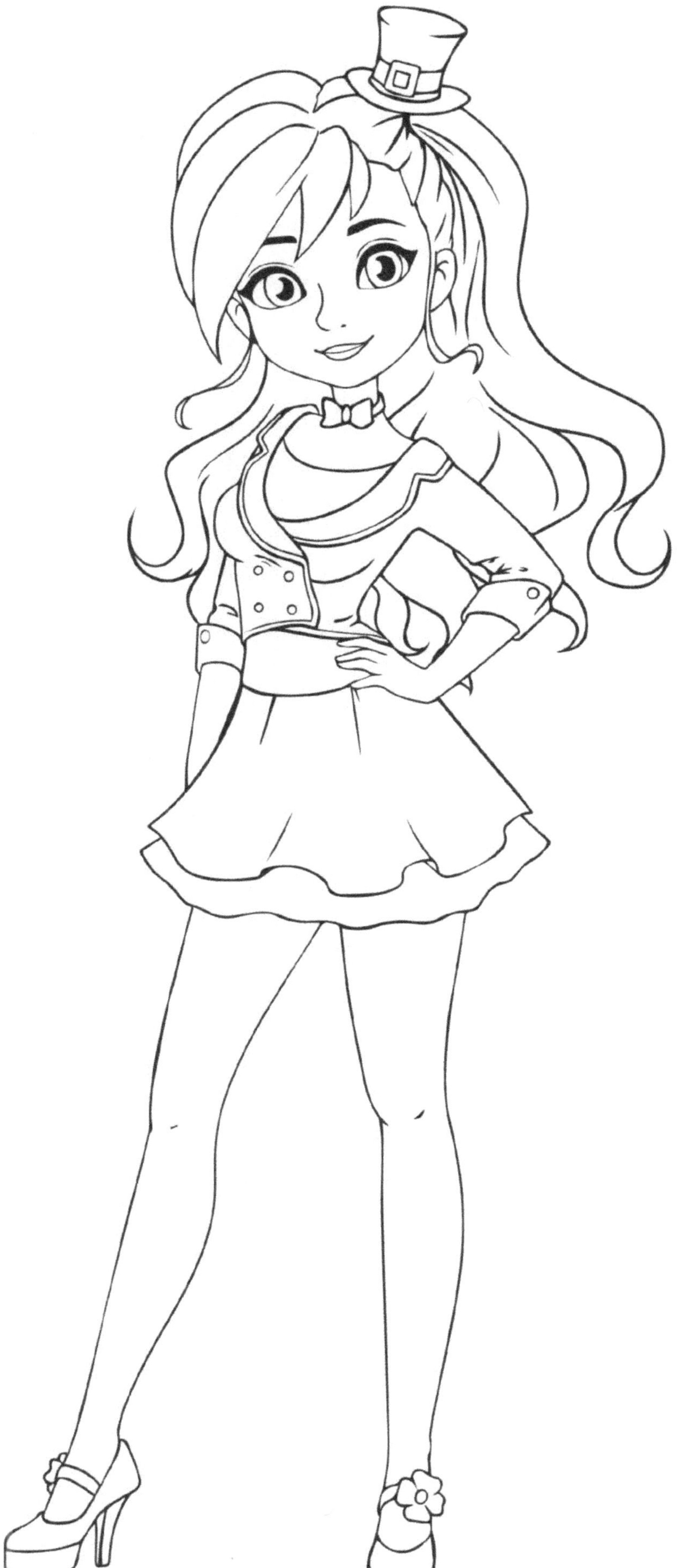

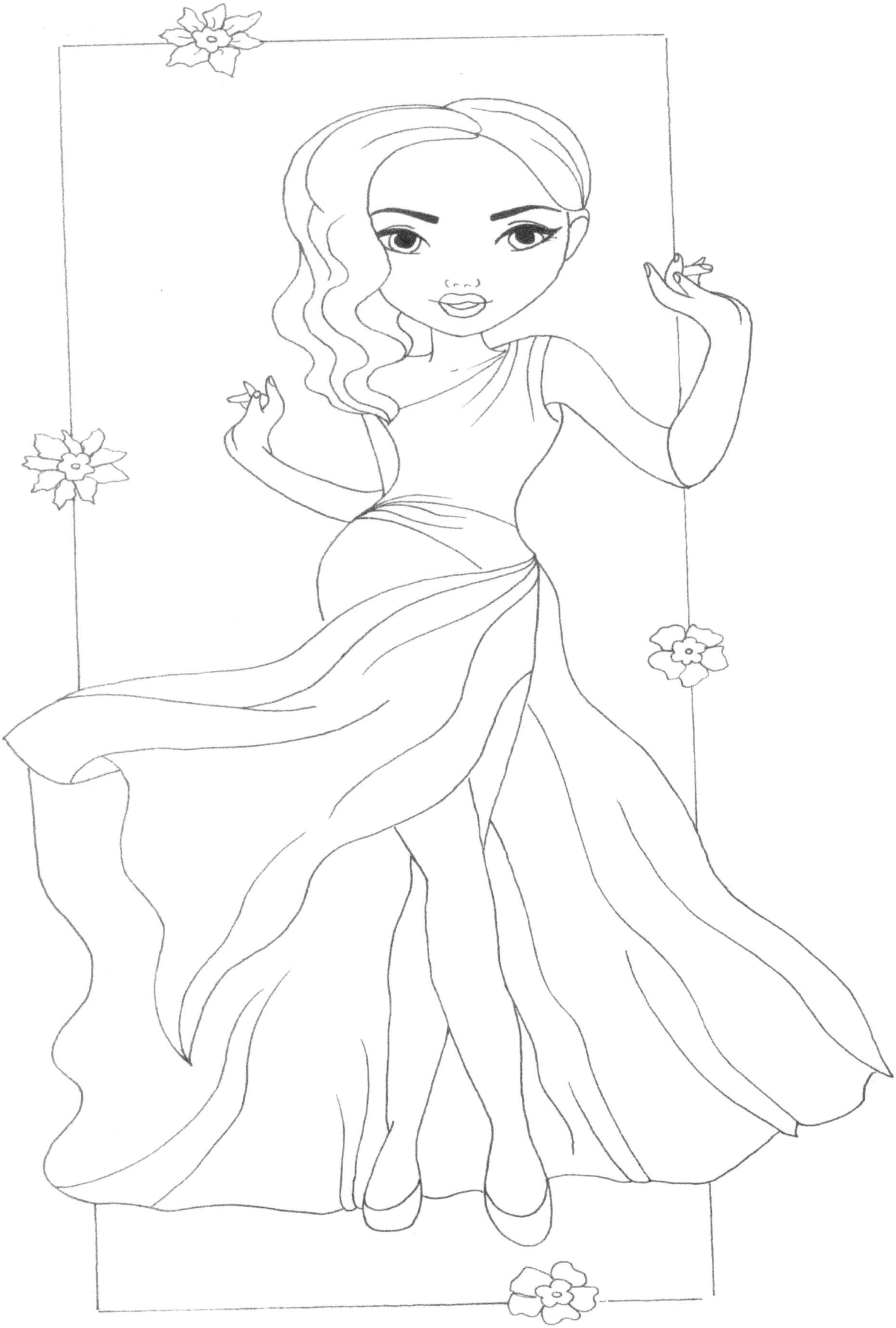

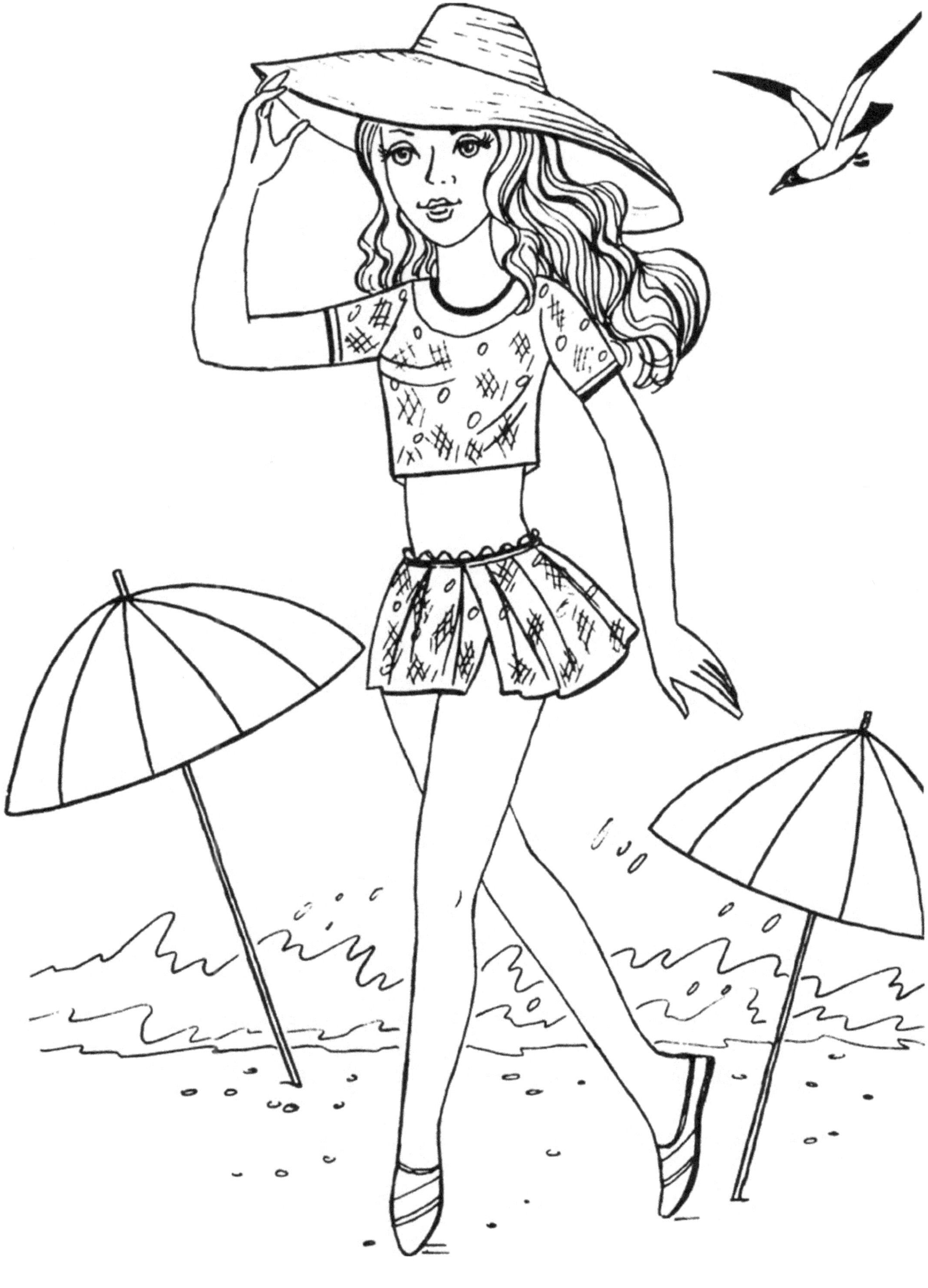

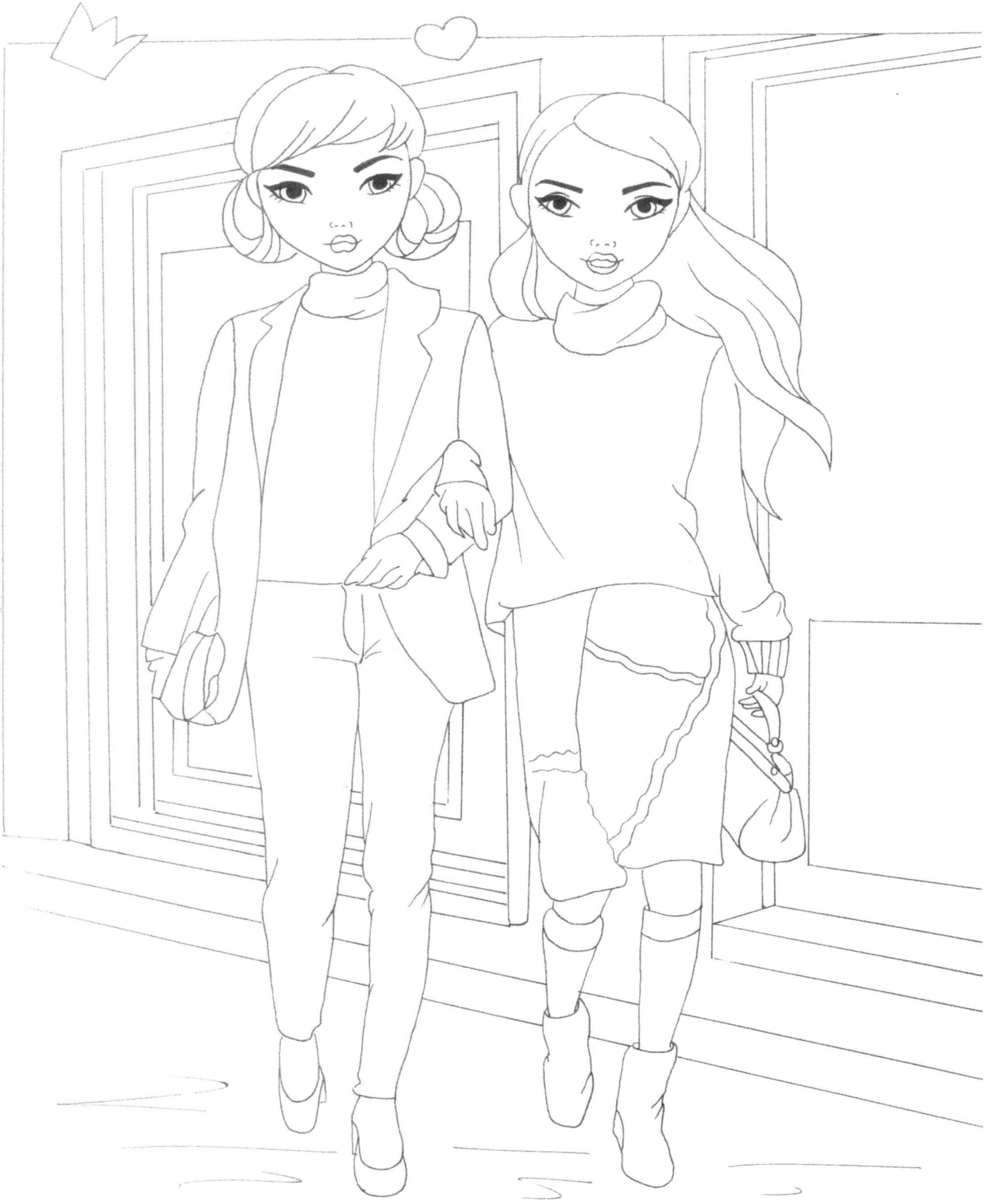

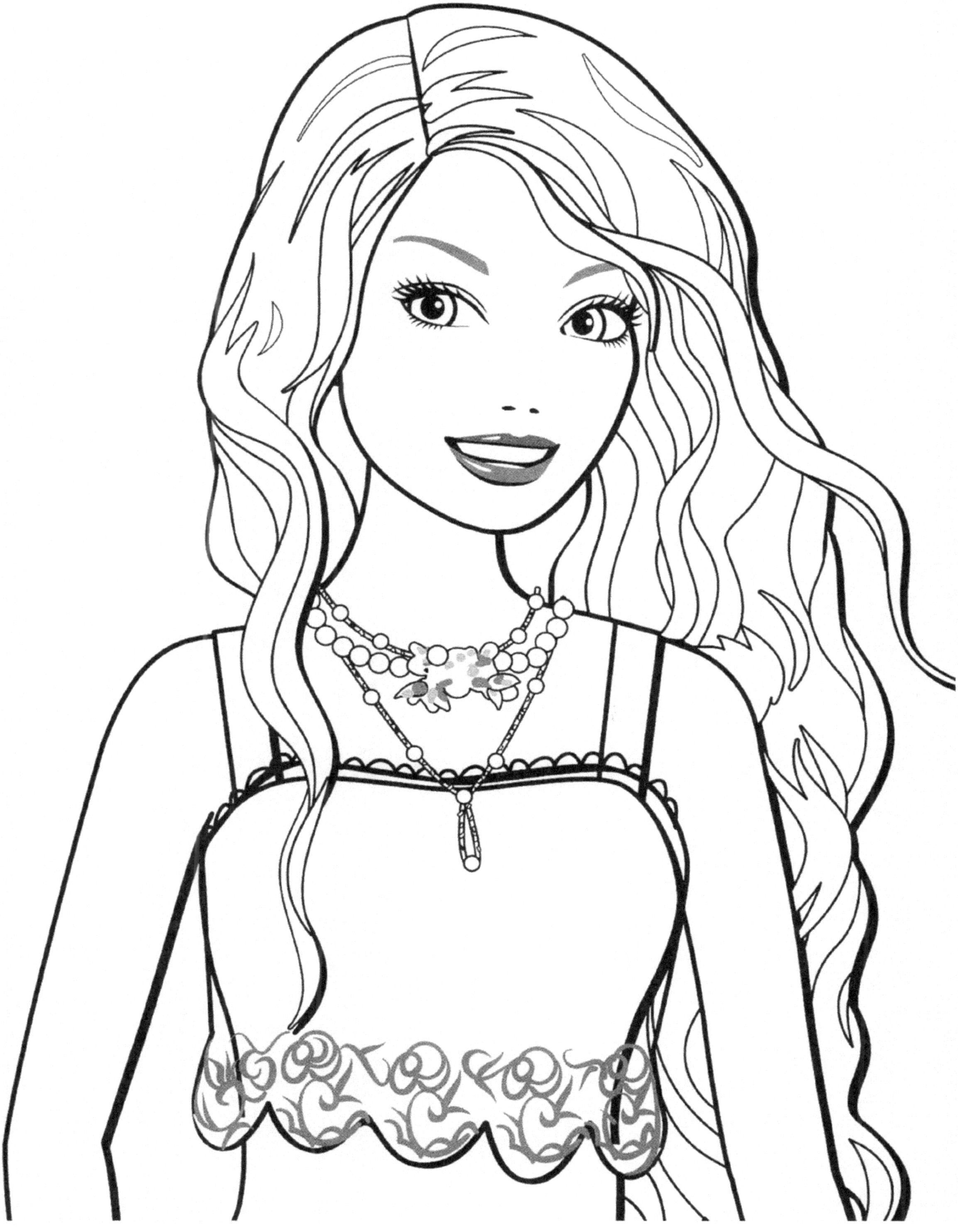

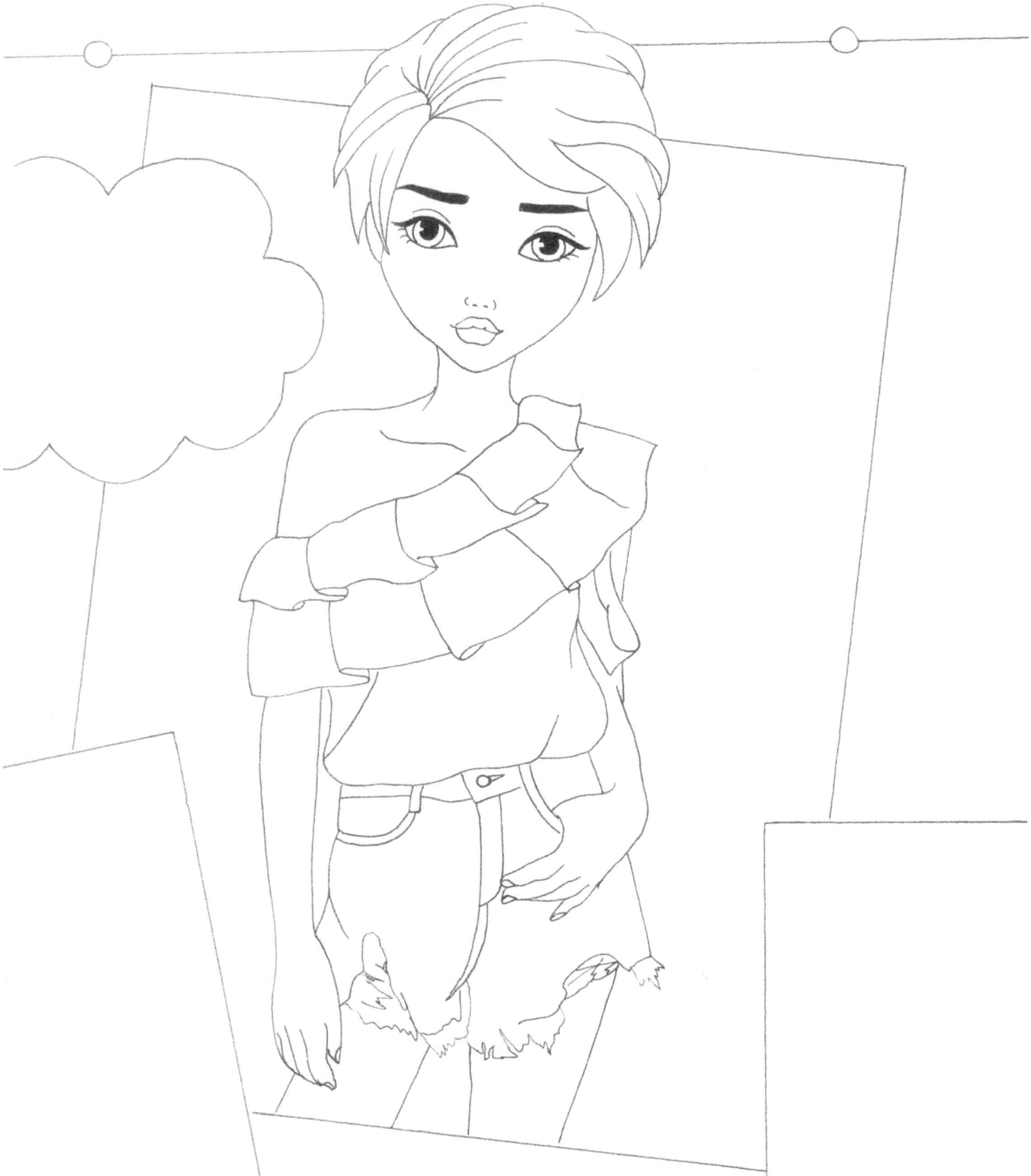

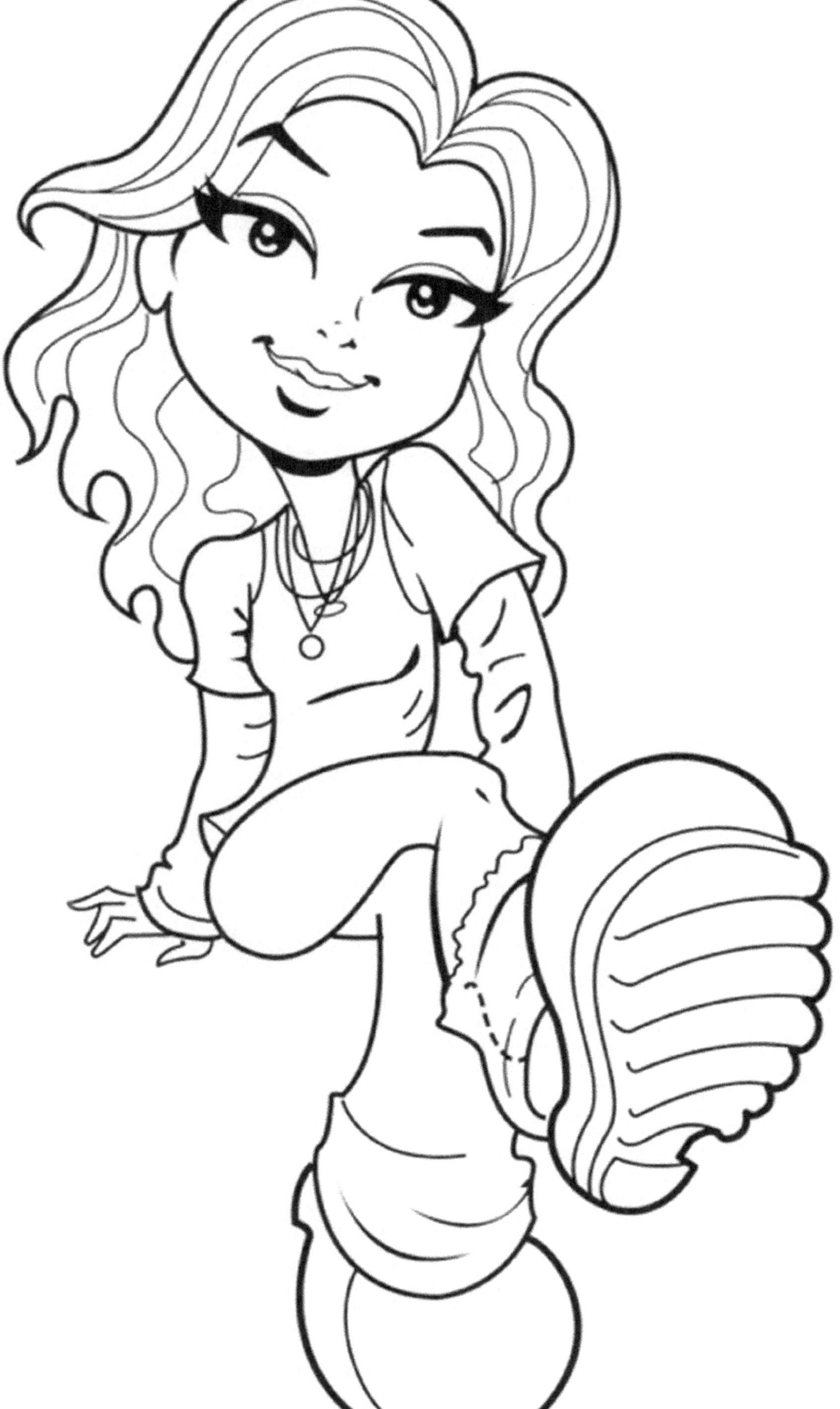

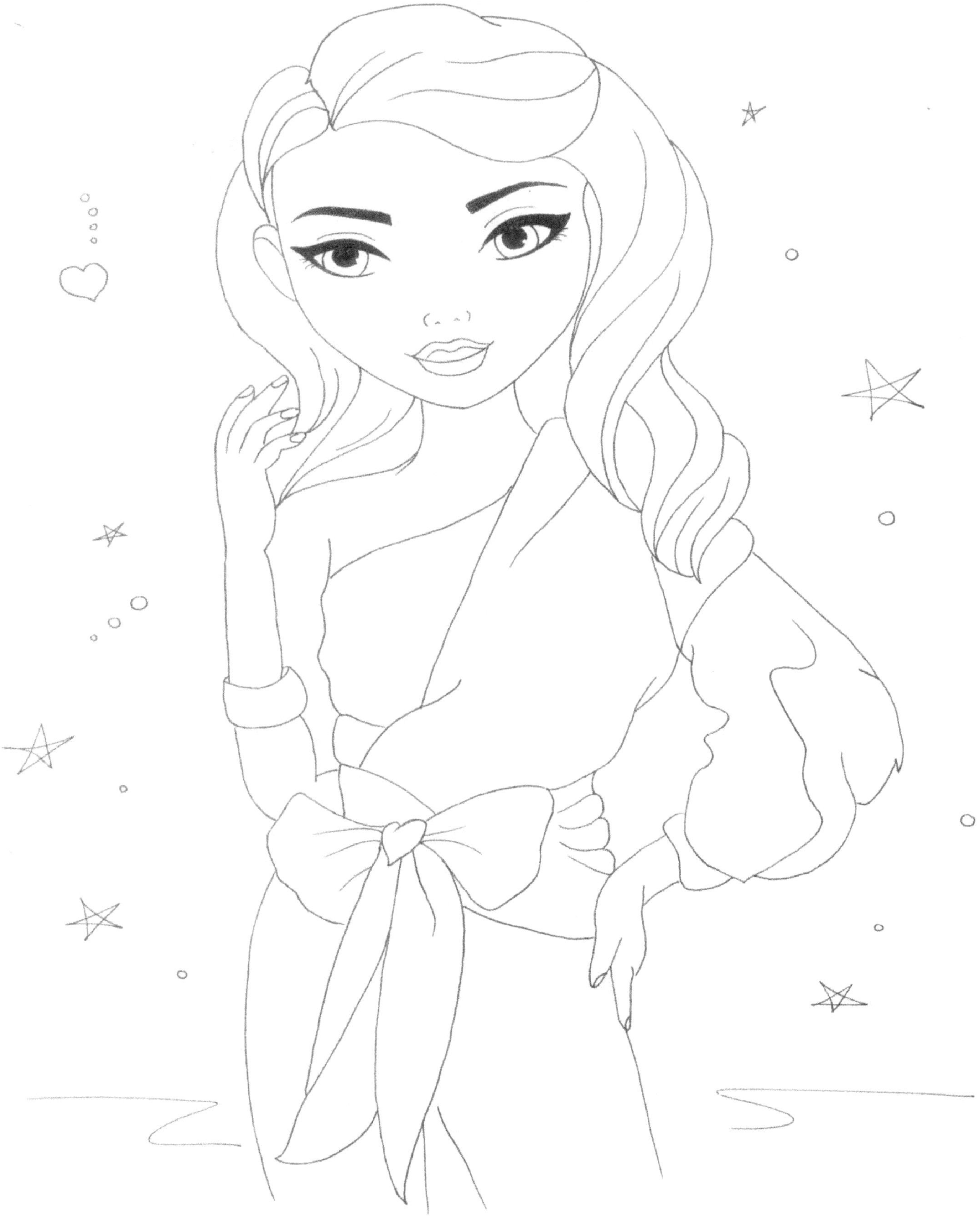

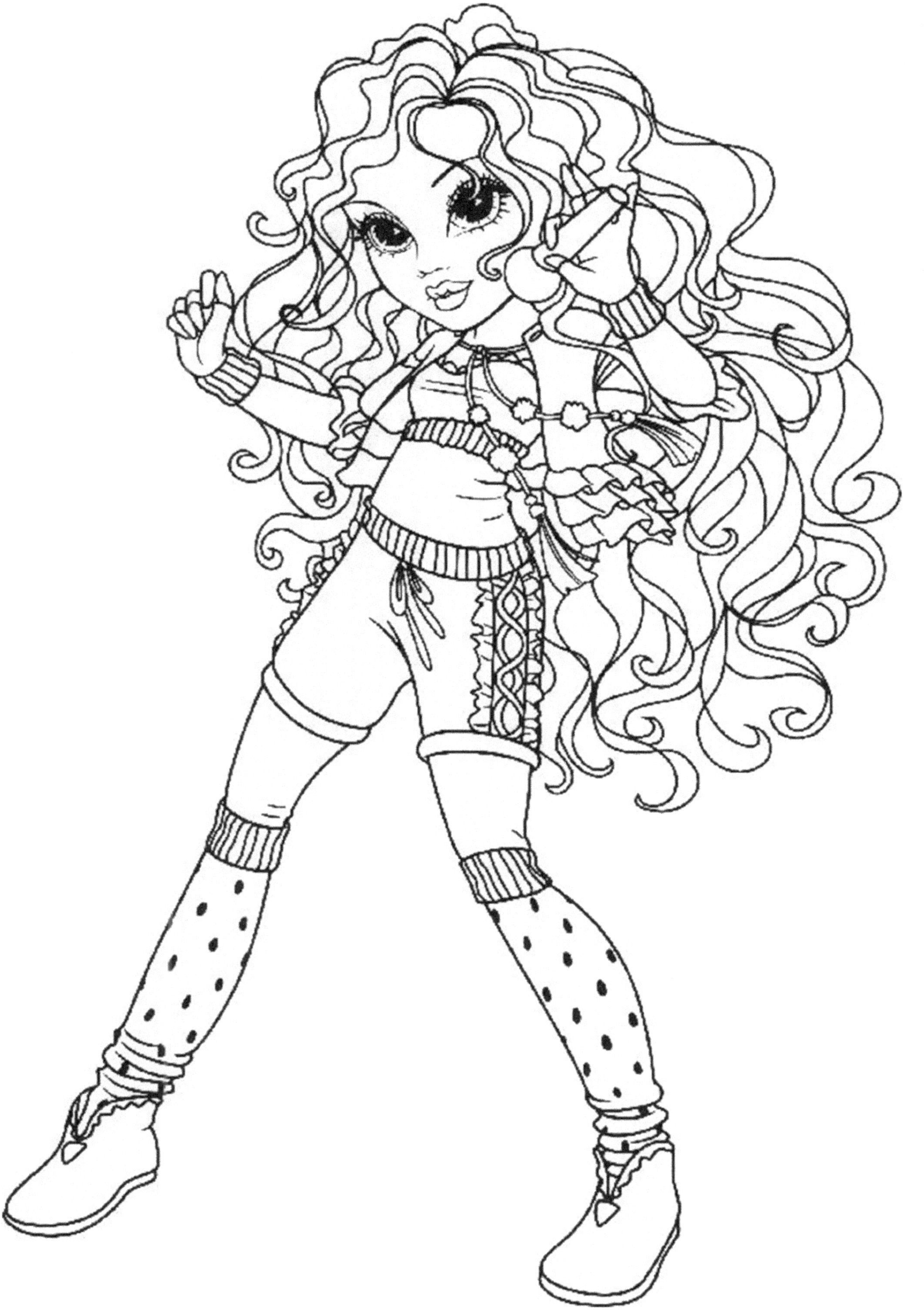

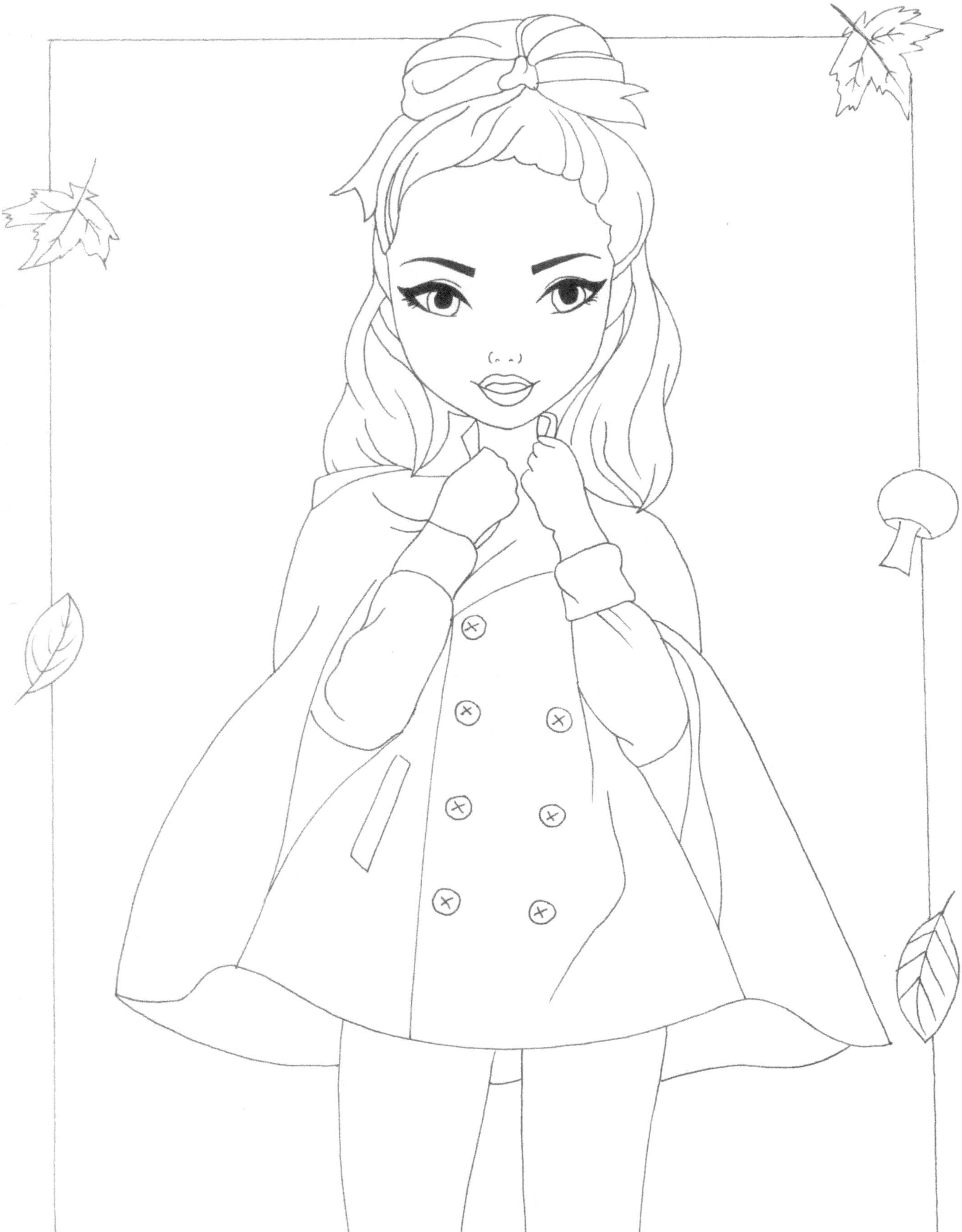

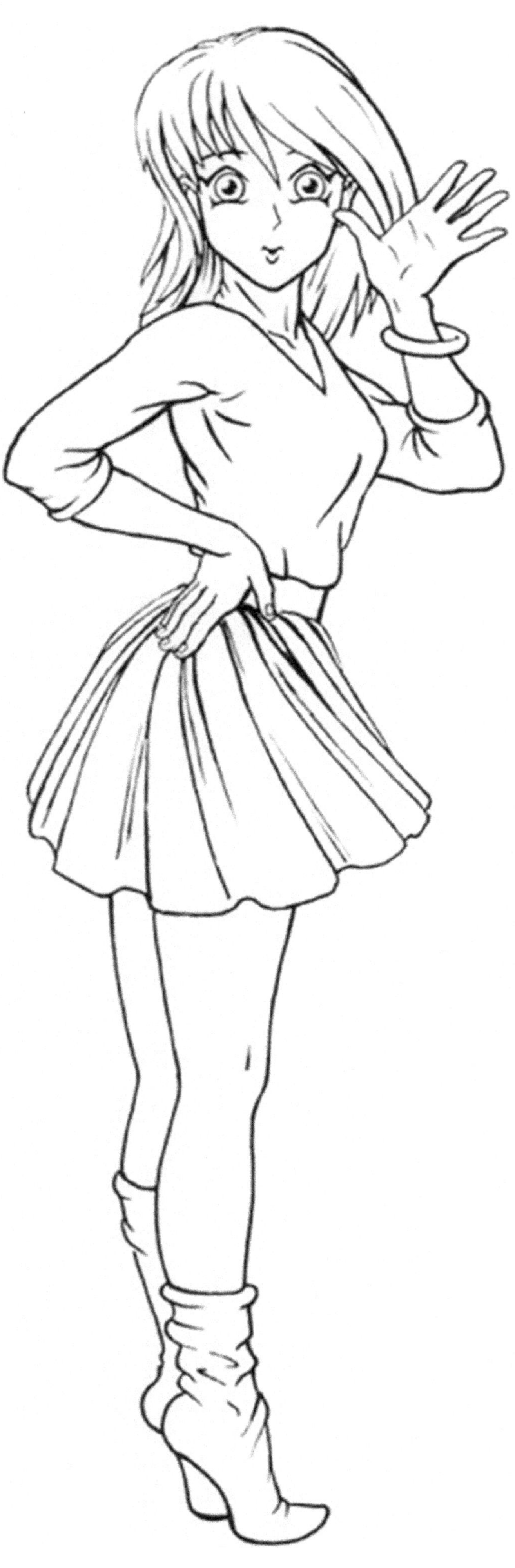

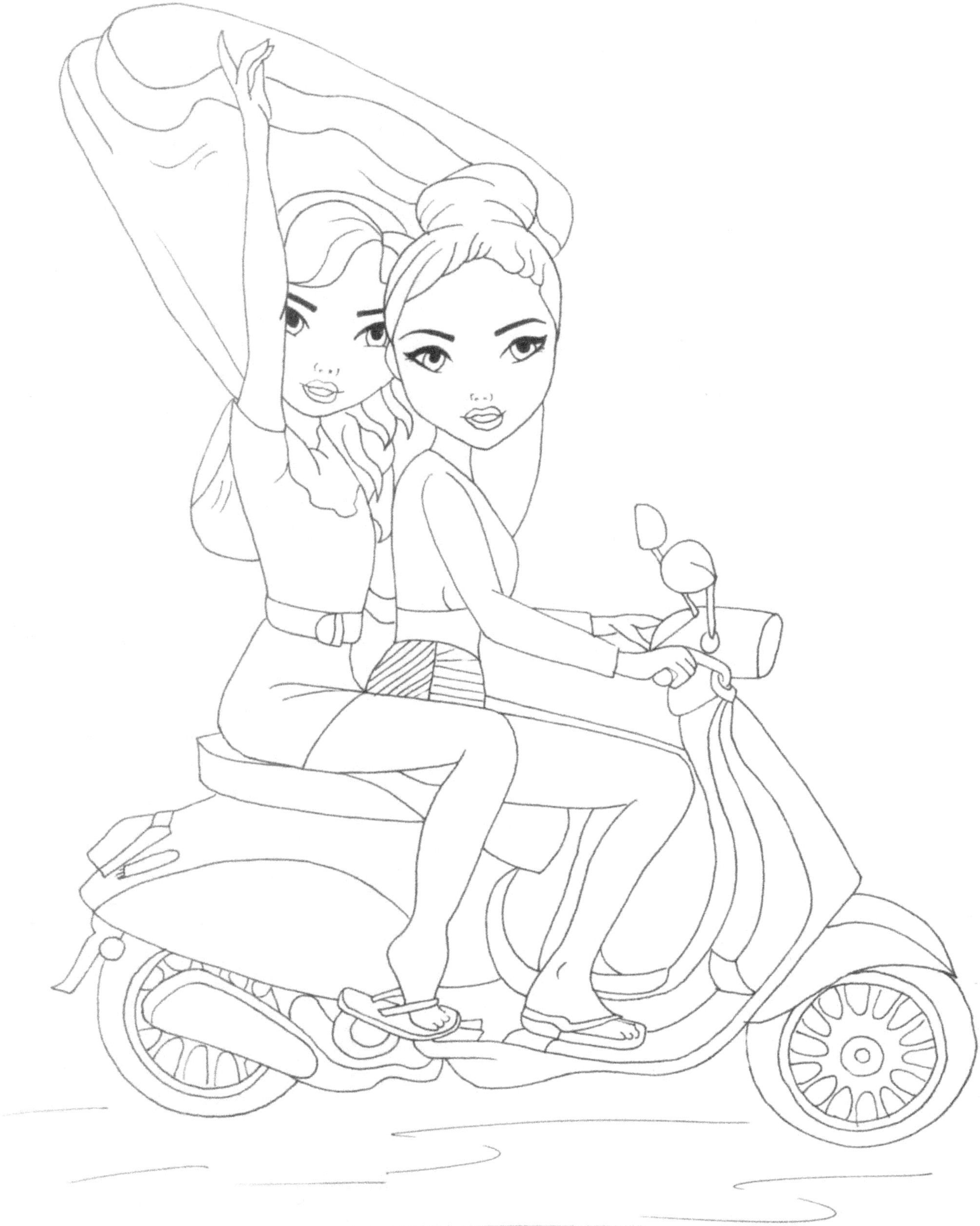

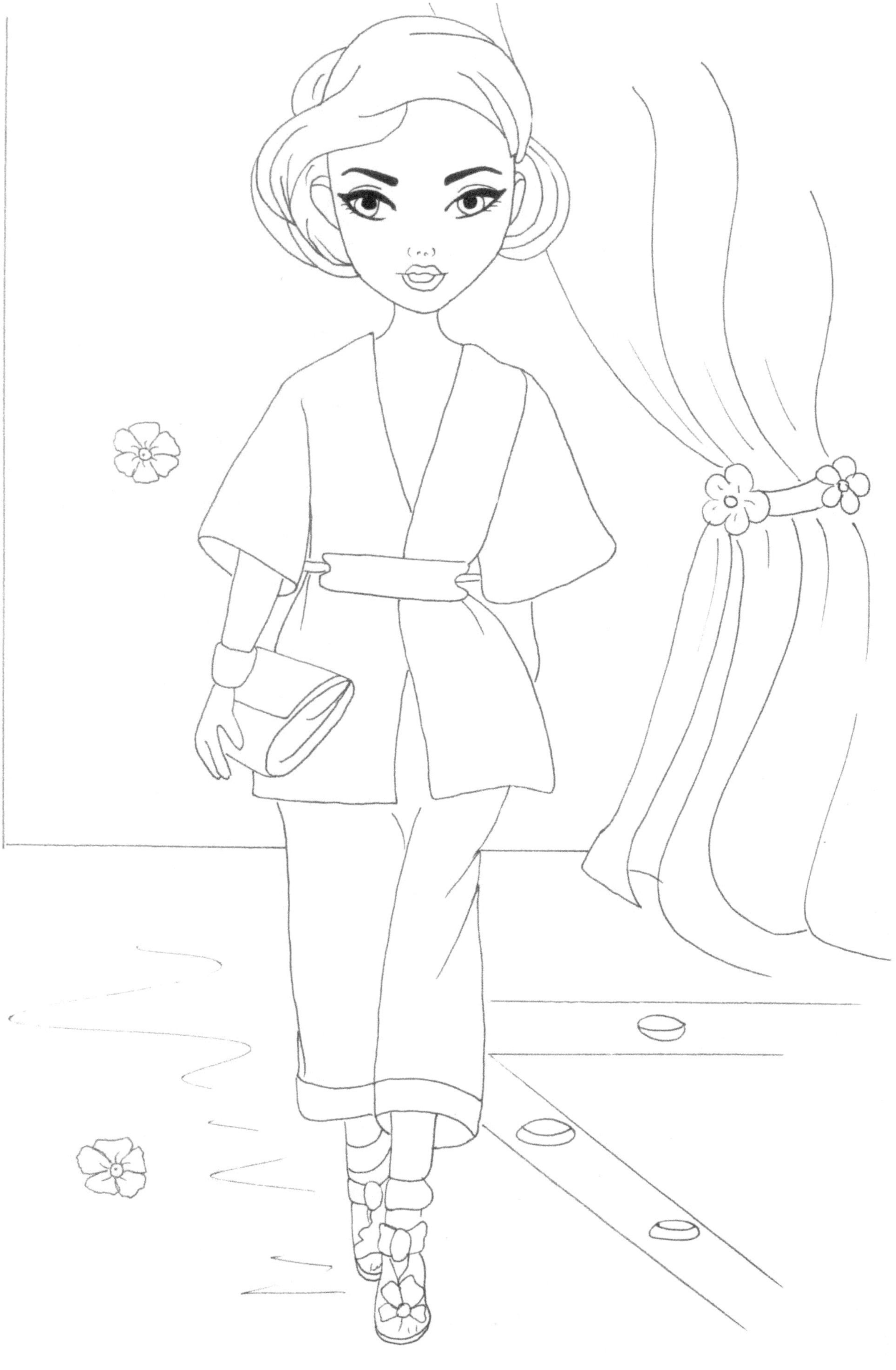

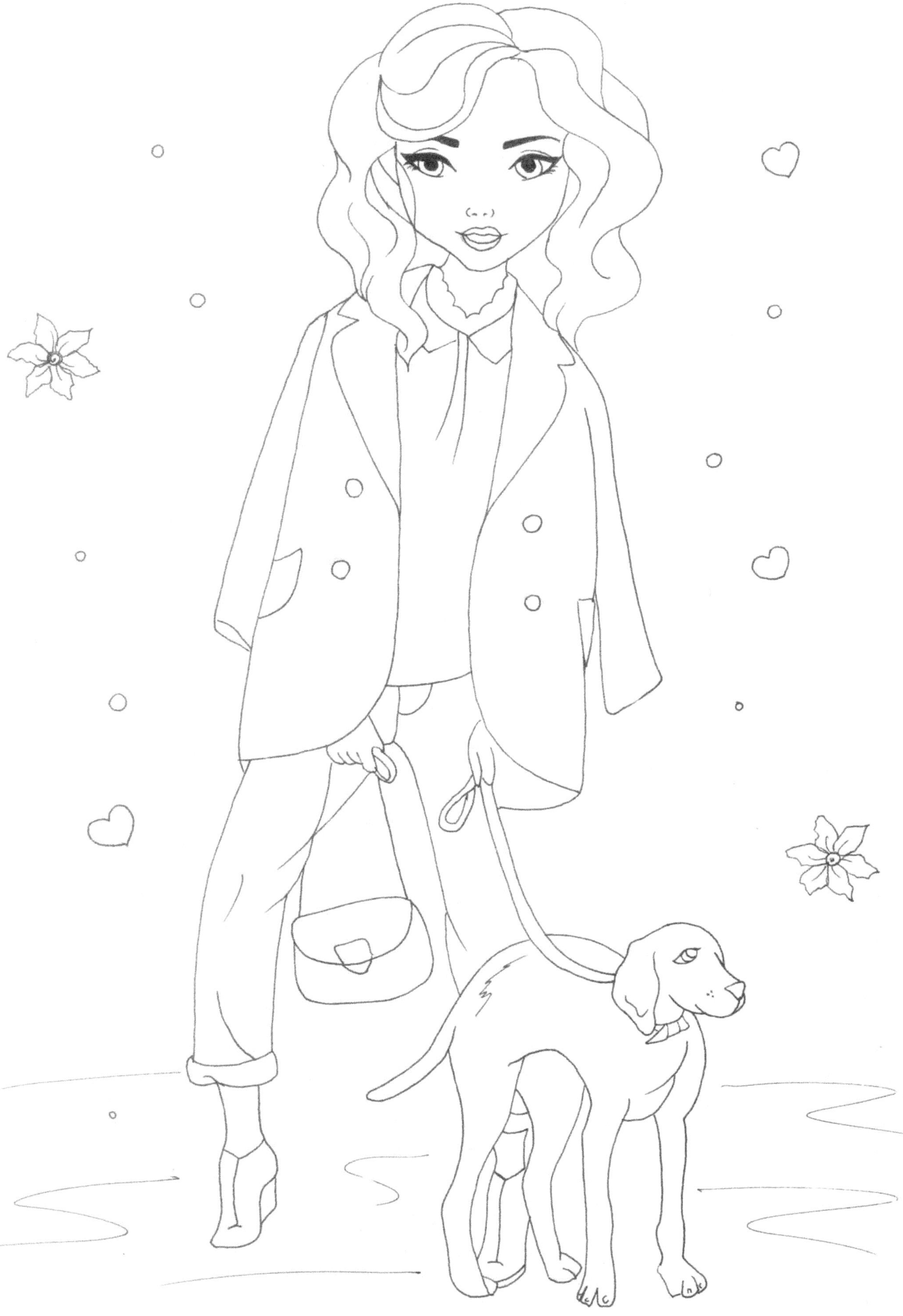

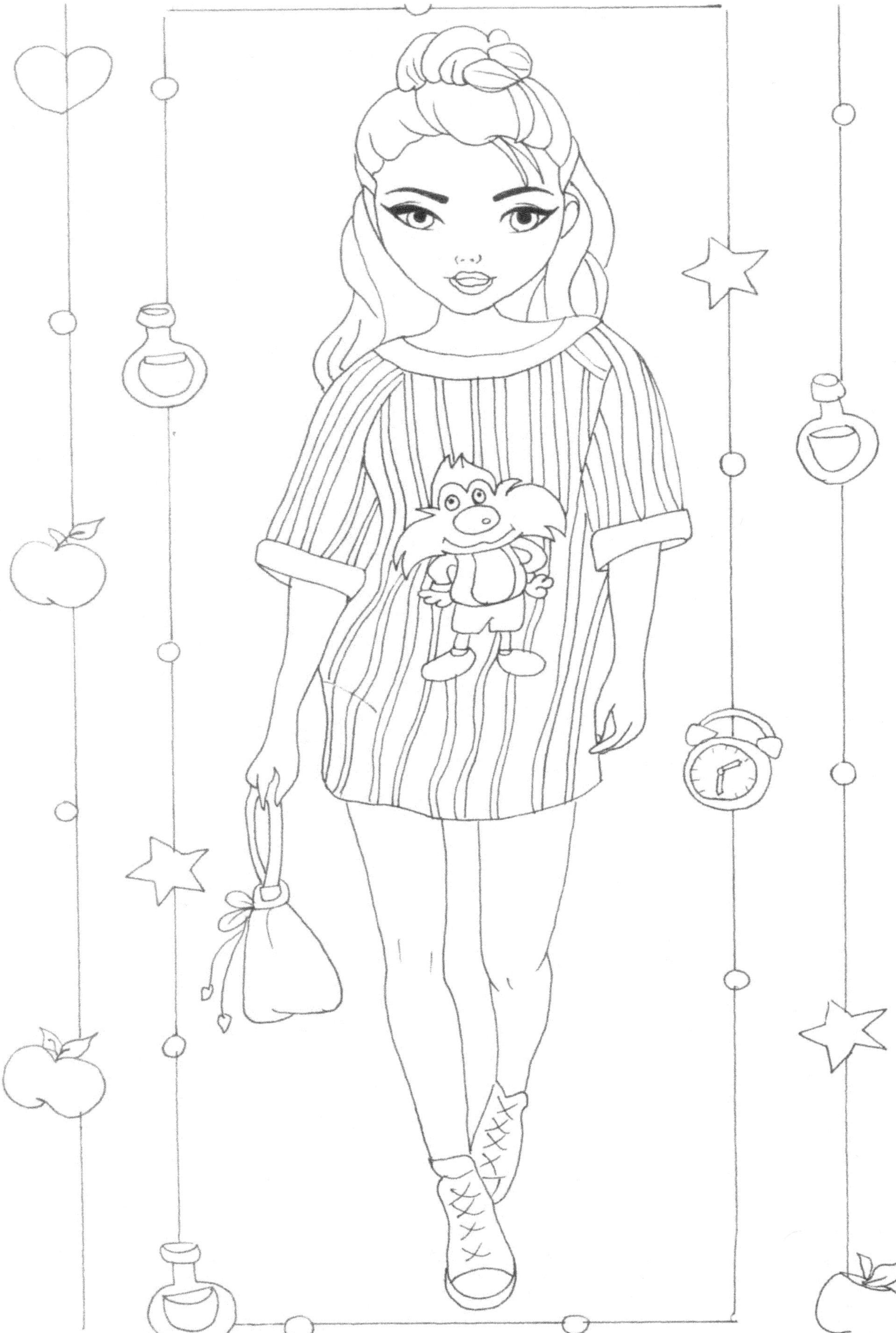

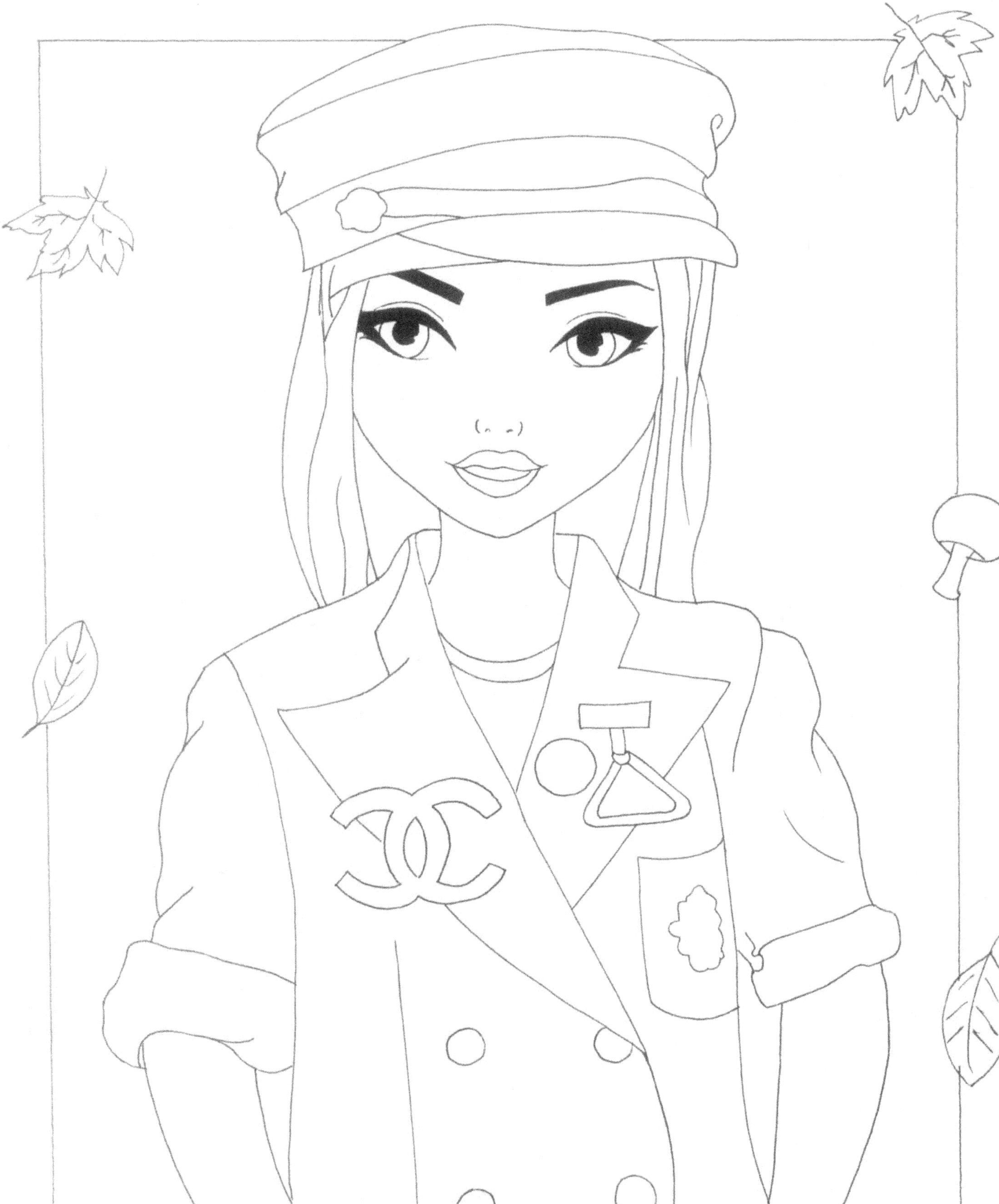

Printed in the USA
CPSIA information can be obtained
at www.ICGtesting.com
LVHW061423211124
797215LV00064BA/907
* 9 7 9 8 6 8 7 5 6 0 9 7 9 *